NET CURTAINS
AND CLOSED DOORS

NET CURTAINS AND CLOSED DOORS

Intimacy, Family, and Public Life in Dublin

Elizabeth A. Throop

BERGIN & GARVEY
Westport, Connecticut • London

Library of Congress Cataloging-in-Publication Data

Throop, Elizabeth A., 1958–
    Net curtains and closed doors : intimacy, family, and public life
in Dublin / Elizabeth A. Throop.
        p.   cm.
    Includes bibliographical references and index.
    ISBN 0–89789–636–X (alk. paper)
    1. Urban anthropology—Ireland—Dublin. 2. City and town life—
Ireland—Dublin. 3. Working class families—Ireland—Dublin.
4. Family—Religious aspects—Catholic Church. 5. Work and family—
Ireland—Dublin. 6. Interpersonal relations and culture—Ireland—
Dublin. 7. Dublin (Ireland)—Social life and customs. I. Title.
GN585.I7T47   1999
307.76'09418'35—dc21   98–51217

British Library Cataloguing in Publication Data is available.

Library of Congress Catalog Card Number: 98–51217
ISBN: 0–89789–636–X

First published in 1999

Bergin & Garvey, 88 Post Road West, Westport, CT 06881
An imprint of Greenwood Publishing Group, Inc.
www.greenwood.com

Printed in the United States of America

The paper used in this book complies with the
Permanent Paper Standard issued by the National
Information Standards Organization (Z39.48–1984).

10 9 8 7 6 5 4 3 2 1

To Catherine Ann Throop (1923–1996)
and
Walter D. Mink, Ph.D. (1928–1996)

Contents

Acknowledgments

I could not have written this book without the help of many people. I would like to thank Dr. Eileen Kane, Dr. Abdullahi El-Tom, and the faculty, students, and staff of the Anthropology Department of St. Patrick's College, Maynooth University, County Kildare; Raphael Kelly; Sheila Power, Dettia O'Reilly, Pat Clarke, and Andy Dillon; Professor Ciáran Benson, Dr. Geraldine Moane, and the students and staff of University College Dublin's Psychology Department; Fionnuala Kilfeather of the National Parents' Council (Primary); Ed McHale and the staff of Clanwilliam Family Institute; Dr. Declan Quigley of Queen's University Belfast; and the Anthropology Association of Ireland. I would also like to thank the Irish families and individuals of "Rathkelly" and points beyond, willing to allow me into their homes and their lives; because I do not want to make you identifiable, I will not name you. But you have enriched my life, and this study, beyond all hopes. I owe you a large and unpayable debt.

Dr. Marc J. Swartz, from the moment we met, has provided friendship and wise support through my personal and intellectual triumphs and travails, and I deeply appreciate him, as I do Audrey Swartz's kindness and good cheer. I also am deeply thankful to the late Professor Walter D. Mink of Macalester College, St. Paul, Minnesota, whose unflagging friendship and scholarship over the past twenty years served as an exemplar for my development as a scholar and as a person. I am grateful as well to Professor Richard Madsen of the Sociology Department at UCSD for his constant support, intellectual stimulation, and friendship; I was delighted to be able to introduce Walt and Dick a few years ago, mentors to me at different parts of my life. Jane Garry, my editor at Greenwood, has become a new and terrific support, and I thank her for her involvement and interest in my work and in me. My friends Dr. Peter Zelles and Linda Snouffer, Jennifer Sils and Mac King, Dr. Lisa Dietrich and John Weinzettle, Leslie and Dr. Mark Slouka, and Pam and Dr. Alex Bolyanatz all have patiently listened to my book-related ramblings, and I thank them for that.

Finally I offer my deepest thanks and appreciation to my parents, Robert and Catherine Ann Throop, for their unflagging support, interest, and love throughout. My mother, Catherine Ann, died as I was completing the first draft of this book; she is very much a part of it.

Though I acknowledge the help and support of many people in the process of researching and writing this book, and though I have received much good advice and information, it is certain that I have made mistakes in data collection and analysis despite the best efforts of my friends and advisors. All errors and misinterpretations are mine alone.

This project was supported in part by a United States Information Service–Fulbright Scholarship (1993–1994) and the University of California–San Diego Anthropology Department Graduate Student Fund (1993–1995); all other parts were self-financed.

Introduction

Anthropology is the art of making the strange familiar and the familiar strange.

Sometime in the mid-1970s, as I was beginning my lifelong fascination with anthropology at age 15, I heard or read this somewhere. It is, by now, a commonplace; most anthropologists have the catch phrase memorized. In this book, I attempt to make the Republic of Ireland—ostensibly a place familiar to many Americans—strange in some ways and familiar in others.

Before I went to Ireland, I believed I knew what Ireland was about. Like almost every American, I have a mixture of nationalities to claim, and as with many Americans, the highest percentage is Irish. (I've met only a few Americans who do not claim some kind of Irish ancestry.) My maternal great-grandmother, Annie Riley, emigrated in the 1850s or 1860s to the United States from (we think) Sligo and married a man, Joseph Kenny, who emigrated from Galway in the early 1850s. Her youngest daughter, my grandmother, Florence Kenny, married a man who was half-Irish and half-Danish (Edward Nelson, changed from "Nielsen" upon his father's arrival in Minnesota). That makes me about

38% Irish—the rest is German and English and, as I've said, Danish. My Anglo-German relatives, though, lived far away from my family as I was growing up, and we strongly identified with the Irish through my mother.

I never understood it, though. I hated the judgmental nature of family gatherings; I feared the colossal drinking of my extended family; I cringed under the sarcasm that we never overtly confronted. My mother told me, as I was growing up, of the various squabbles within her family of origin, and I simply couldn't comprehend why my mother endured what she did for the sake of family peace. I was too American, I guess, and perhaps too baby-boomer: I tended to face issues squarely rather than keep the peace. It wasn't until a couple of years before her death that my mother began asserting herself in a way atypical for an Irish person (even though she was third-generation Irish American).

Luckily, we didn't see the extended family all that much. But they formed, in part, a picture for me of the people who I would encounter during my research in Ireland. Like many Irish Americans, as I anticipated my first trip to Ireland (a holiday in 1990), I expected fey, whimsical, and sardonic folk with a liking for the drop. Unlike many Irish Americans, I had the privilege to live in Ireland long enough (from September 1993 to March 1995) to discard that colonialist, patronizing image. I found a sophisticated European city in Dublin—granted, with pubs at the hub of many social networks, but there was little whimsy and a good deal of energy, subtle humor, and cosmopolitan analysis of the United States and the world. I found some wonderful friends. I met some clearly dysfunctional, unpleasant folks. I spent time with a number of different kinds of people: unmarried or separated men and women, single parents, gay men and lesbian women, married couples and, oftentimes, their families, children, university students, elderly people, Americans, English, Arabs, Africans, Australians, Scots, Germans—but almost all of my time was spent in the company of Irish people.

I learned the truth of the old *pishogue*: "You've two ears and one mouth for a very good reason: to listen twice as much as you speak." One cannot be an adequate ethnographer unless that proverb is heeded. Indeed, this is especially important in Ireland, as I demonstrate in this book. I discovered early on that a primary cultural understanding is that it is highly improper to discuss oneself, one's feelings, one's health, one's thoughts, or even one's day beyond a brief mention. To do more than this is to be greedy and selfish, to draw too much attention to oneself. I'm sure that my Irish friends and informants will find this introduction typically American and self-serving especially as I say that I found this part of Irish culture, so very different from American braggadocio and self-revelatory culture, exhausting and frustrating.

In this book, which is drawn from my doctoral dissertation, I discuss Irish culture in the context of its history, social structures, cultural understandings regarding family life and emotional intimacy, and typical experiences along a continuum of public life and private life. I am an anthropologist, but I also call upon many other disciplines to illuminate Irish culture. I am largely empirical in my approach in that I do not believe that I have "created" Irish culture as I have written it down—I am not entirely sympathetic to what I will gloss as the "postmodern" approach to anthropology. I provide no narratives, no discourse analysis, and little of myself in the body of this book. I see that societies have patterns of behaviors that are guided by culture; that I see some of the same patterns in 1990s Dublin as Nancy Scheper-Hughes (1979) saw in rural 1970s Kerry tells me of the persistence of cultural patterns (I differ from Scheper-Hughes's interpretations of these behaviors, however). At the same time, I am not convinced that anthropology is a "science" in the sense that chemistry, for instance, is a science. I cannot help but interpret behavior with my own cultural lenses, my own experiences, my gender, my sense of power, my nationality and ethnicities. The observer does affect the observed, but part of that observed includes consistent patterns of behaviors, thoughts, and emotions guided by culture. I am guided as an anthropologist by notions of relativity but also ideas of consistency. I am neither completely an objective scientist nor a totally subjective narrator.

I base my analysis of Irish culture on information collected during a fieldwork period of September 1993 to March 1995. Almost all data were gathered during participant observation, though my research assistant, James Kinsella, designed and distributed an unsupervised self-administered questionnaire in winter and spring 1994 regarding cultural understandings about marriage and family. I did all tabulations and analysis of the questionnaire; I found the questions and results to be too general to be of use except as primarily background information.

My informant base consisted primarily of working-class families[1] or segments thereof (for example, separated men and women) in Dublin and, to a lesser extent, Limerick and a large town in County Kildare, which I don't name for confidentiality reasons. However, I had more informal contact with a number of middle-class individuals and informants, many of whom were reared in working-class or rural families. I discuss both working-class and middle-class role relationships in this study.

In the second half of my fieldwork, I focused on five Dublin-area working-class families, visiting with each in their homes at least once a week for five or six hours. Sometimes children were present; more often they were not. Often—particularly during holiday periods—we met more frequently. One-on-one interviews were usually conducted during an afternoon tea drinking or evening pub session. Almost all information was gathered in informants' houses, at pubs or coffee shops, or when informants visited my flat.

I was introduced to families through faculty and students of the Anthropology Department, St. Patrick's College, Maynooth, County Kildare; the National Parents' Council (a voluntary parents' organization concerned with the state of primary and secondary school education); Clanwilliam Institute;[2] and students of the Psychology Department, University College Dublin. Neighbors in Castleknock and Ranelagh provided further information and access to their experience, and fellow Fulbright recipients introduced me to several casual informants as well. In addition, a priest friend in Limerick allowed me to interview a number of his parishioners.

Most of the families with whom I worked welcomed me in immediately. After two or three meetings, they seemed comfortable with my presence. Occasionally, I would arrive in the middle of a flaming row;[3] I knew I was, more or less, part of the family when the row continued. Another marker was when I was the person responsible for making the tea; in fact, one family devised a schedule of tea-making responsibilities and included me in that schedule.

I must make clear (and I will continue to do so throughout the book) that I have altered all names, neighborhood locations, and biographical details of the persons I describe in this book. In many cases, when identifying details of a specific person would be too obvious, I combined the identities of informants. However, all direct quotes are, in fact, direct: an actual person conforming to the identity I attached to her or him spoke the words I provide in the situations I describe. The Irish people I came to know and respect had strong and reasonable concerns about anonymity, as did I, since they were revealing so much of their lives to me. Indeed, most recoiled when I called them "informants," as the term was uncomfortably close to the hated identity "informer," despised in a country colonized for so long.

I also want to state that many of my friends and informants told me far more than I repeat here. I leave those very personal and emotionally difficult stories out because of my own ethical and moral concerns about preserving the dignity of the people who helped me understand Irish culture and themselves as individuals. I felt privileged to hear my friends' troubles and have not, I hope, broken their trust. Any stories I tell here are stories that are known by others in a person's network; they are more or less "public."

And that is where the tale begins. I have never been easy with simple dichotomies. Starkly drawn lines between black and white, either/or, right and wrong, scientific and empirical, male and female, yes and no, public and private trouble me. Life simply doesn't work this way, in my experience. Yet as I began my graduate studies in anthropology after a decade in the work force (as a family therapist and a paralegal), I read the old anthropological stalwarts as they declared that scientific anthropological analysis showed that "public" experience was fundamentally different from "private" life. Not too surprisingly, the old stalwarts were almost all white European or American men; not too surprisingly, they were far more interested in "public" life, which seemingly involved men far more than women; not too surprisingly, I disagreed even before beginning to read those studies conventionally grouped under "feminist" anthropology. I could not believe that major spheres of life—the family and economic activities, for instance—were so completely opposed. It certainly hadn't been my experience, either in my own life or in the lives of my family and friends. I also didn't think that my experience as a woman somehow connected me in a special and wonderful way to a heightened sense of connection between the various arenas of my life. Neither the old stalwarts nor the more radical feminists made sense to me.

The more reasonable explanation had to lie somewhere in between, I thought. And one way to demonstrate that would be to investigate a familiar yet strange culture, one that was Western (whatever that means) but that also wasn't, one that was urban but also wasn't. Ireland, a society firmly grounded in some Euro-American cultural understandings while remaining culturally distinct, seemed a good place to be exploring such things—especially since no one had ever done an ethnographic study of Dublin.

I went to Ireland expecting complexity rather than simplicity. I was not disappointed. I found a vibrant, sardonic, self-critical set of people who, quite rightly, resented Americans who came over to "analyze" them. The Irish people I came to know were still smarting from Scheper-Hughes's treatment (1979) of them as psychopathological, though they were continually bothered by Americans' pronouncements on Dubliners and Irish culture based on, apparently, brief stays in Dublin. It took some time for people to believe that I would not paint similar pictures, that I appreciated the strengths as well as the limitations of Irish culture and society.

So the purposes of this book are severalfold. One of my aims included a scholarly one of providing an accurate ethnographic account of urban Ireland, something that hasn't been done previously; instead, all discussions of Ireland have involved deeply rural and largely government-supported Irish-language (*Gaeltacht*) areas (see Chapter 4). Second, I intended to provide information for those of us living outside Ireland who call ourselves Irish. In part, I hoped to show that the sentimental "memories" of Ireland held by many descendants of Irish immigrants have little to do with twenty-first-century Ireland. Third, I undertook to demonstrate that the conventional and scholarly understandings of a common dichotomy—public and private—did not conform to lived experience in a Western society in the way the dichotomy is discussed.

Softening the public/private dichotomy potentially has tremendous impact beyond the academy. For instance, I argue that the family is not and never really has been a bastion of relationships fundamentally different than those in other arenas of life no matter in which society one lives. (In fact, the notion that the "nuclear family" is somehow the only traditional and natural domestic form is a peculiarly American idea; Stephanie Coontz [1992] demonstrates that the nuclear family, for most of America's history, has not been economically, emotionally, and socially viable.) If I am right that the family does not work in isolation, current calls to get "big government" out of our "private" lives fall flat. I discuss this further at the end of this book.

Suffice it to say that my account of Ireland shows us a place no longer ruled by the Little People, by fairies and leprechauns—if it ever was such a place. Ireland and its cities are very much a part of the postindustrial world, participating in the world at large with exquisite sensitivity and perceptive skill. Indeed, the Irish seem to understand the world economy far better than do Americans even as they maintain a sense of responsibility, through a social welfare system for all citizens, to each other.

Many people helped me try to grasp some parts of Irish culture. I hope their trust in me has been justified.

NOTES

1. No figures are available that specify percentages of working-class workers to middle-class workers. However, 1987 statistics indicate that 15.2% of the workforce is in agriculture, 27.8% is in industry, and 57.1% is in services (*European Communities Encyclopedia and Directory* 1992:137). Informants consider industrial workers to be working class if they are not managerial; most service workers are shop clerks, hairdressers, nonmanagerial civil servants (telephone linemen, for example), and other nonprofessional workers without postsecondary school education.

2. No families discussed within this study were part of the client population at Clanwilliam Institute owing to entirely appropriate therapeutic confidentiality concerns on the part of the staff there. I was allowed to observe sessions conducted by family therapists, and I participated in some treatment planning since I hold an M.S.W. and had worked as a family therapist with violent and incestuous families in the mid-1980s in Chicago. These therapy and planning

sessions serve as background information in my analysis, particularly concerning marital and child-rearing issues.

3. A "row," pronounced to rhyme with "cow," is Irish English for an argument.

CHAPTER 1

Public and Private Domains: The Social Science View

THE BLEND OF PUBLIC AND PRIVATE EXPERIENCE

Most social relationships blend elements of cultural understandings regarding the nature of public life and private life rather than act as mutually exclusive social domains. Some interactions can be seen as almost solely public or nearly completely private, but most of social life is much more muddy. In this study, I examine the blend of public and private elements of relationships, using Irish social interaction in the family and other social arenas as an illustrative case. Through a delineation of some statuses and associated role relationships held by Irish men and women, I demonstrate that current scholarly work preserving a strict dichotomous view of public and private life does not always account for human behavior and experience.

In this first chapter, I argue that most researchers claiming to identify the connections between public and private do not specify exactly how public and private are intertwined, something I do in this book. Scholars do not generally advance precise definitions of public and private. Instead, there is a general assumption that the private equals the family and the public is everything else (Hochschild 1983:69; Morgan 1975:4; Coontz 1992:125). I establish that this strict dichotomy has a long history in Western social thought and in anthropology, and I provide some definitions that I use in later chapters. I then look at some of the literature that deals with the issues of public and private life most often, that of the sociology, history, and anthropology of the family. I contend that the actual social mechanisms used by people as they blend elements of public and private cultural understandings in their relationships are not described in this scholarly literature dealing with the public/private dichotomy. Ethnographic analysis dealing with the worlds of work inadvertently shows the interpenetration of public and private understandings, and I summarize some of that literature. Throughout this study, I illustrate the interpenetration of public and private aspects of social relationships through an analysis of Irish mothers and fathers.

THE PUBLIC/PRIVATE DICHOTOMY IN WESTERN SOCIAL THEORY AND SOCIAL SCIENCE

The notion that public life is a separate domain from family or domestic life is one of the West's oldest philosophical truths. Meyer Fortes, discussed more fully below, notes that Aristotle differentiated between *oikos*, the family in its domestic setting, and *polis*, civil society (Fortes 1969:100). Family life then, for Aristotle, is a fundamentally different experience than is public, political life; neither influences social processes in the other to any significant degree. We can see Aristotle's distinction in the work of social theorists upon whom anthropologists have relied for subsequent analysis of public and private life.

Ferdinand Toennies, for instance, describes *gemeinschaft* and *gesellschaft* as two essentially different social conditions. Gemeinschaft, for Toennies, is community, the affective, intimate world of the family, substantially different in nature from gesellschaft, the public world of contracts, business, and scientific endeavor (Toennies 1961:193–196). Gemeinschaft is instinctual, bound in tradition, and organic, tied to naturally occurring behavior, based on a unity of will of community (Toennies 1961:197–198). For Toennies, the two are fundamentally separate ways of living and organizing social relations.

Emile Durkheim, like Toennies, identifies two separate forms of social organization as mechanical and organic (Durkheim 1961:212–213). A society in which there is little occupational specialization, in which an individual consciousness is little differentiated from the collective conscious, for Durkheim, characterizes mechanical functioning. Mechanical solidarity is that social experience in which each individual is very much like all other individuals; one person does not change the larger society and its shared cultural understandings much. In contrast to this, Durkheim identifies a highly specialized society as organic, in that growth and diversity in the individual promotes growth and diversity in the society. The two—a collective community and an individualized society—are very different. In one, all life is public. The other clearly demarcates individual and societal actions (Durkheim 1961: 212–213).

Similarly, Max Weber distinguishes between associative and communal relationships (Weber 1961:219). Associative relationships are based on rational, individual self-interest, contractual in nature and most often voluntary. Communal relationships, on the other hand, are "based on a subjective feeling of the parties, whether affective or traditional, that they belong together" (Weber 1961:218–219). Associative relationships are social, public, economic, and (or) political; communal relationships are emotionally based, private, and intimate. The two, for Weber, as for Toennies and Durkheim, are fundamentally different and separate. Public life and private life, for these social theorists, stand in opposition.

Some anthropologists continued this tradition, seeing political life as separate from intimate relations in discussing culture and society. E. E. Evans-Pritchard, for example, contends that intimate relationships do not have importance in his analysis of Nuer political life: "Social ties in domestic groups are primarily of a kinship nature . . . [they] do not form part of segmentary systems," and they are not of a political nature (Evans-Pritchard 1940:5–6). For Evans-Pritchard, political life and domestic life are analytically two separate spheres. Domestic relationships, for Evans-Pritchard, are of a qualitatively different order: "The relations between the sexes and between children and adults belong rather to an account of domestic relations rather than to a study of political institutions" (Evans-Pritchard 1940:178). Oikos and polis do not meet analytically for Evans-Pritchard. It appears that he believes that the two domains do not share important qualities or have much effect on each other. Interestingly, though, Evans-Pritchard notes that Nuer women occasionally beat their husbands, with economic and political ramifications that go beyond the household (Evans-Pritchard 1951:104); surely this is an instance in which public and private concerns might be connected, despite Evans-Pritchard's assertion that they are not.

Although A. R. Radcliffe-Brown discusses kinship, ostensibly the result of marriage and family life, he also analytically distinguishes between kinship relations which have "social" ends and those relations of the elementary (nuclear) family group. He too sees a significant difference between oikos and polis. Radcliffe-Brown assumes that behavior within the nuclear family has emotional motivations which lead to like behavior beyond the domestic sphere. For instance, Radcliffe-Brown analyzes the warm relations which often obtain between mother's brother and sister's son, asserting that Ego's affectionate treatment of his mother's brother arises from Ego's warm and loving relationship with his own mother: "The pattern of behaviour toward the mother, which is developed within the family by reason of the nature of the family group and its social life, is extended with suitable modification to the mother's sister and to the mother's brother, then to the group of maternal kindred as a whole, and finally to the maternal gods, the ancestors of the mother's group" (Radcliffe-Brown 1965:27). What is interesting to Radcliffe-Brown is the fact that affection is extended. Questions about the "nature of the family group and its social life" are not addressed. Although Radcliffe-Brown asserts that domestic relations influence extradomestic life, he does not discuss how that influence occurs, leaving unattended the psychosociological processes of extension of maternal affection.

Although Fortes investigates the affective ties that bring kin together, he also treats the elementary family, the domestic group, as not political, social, or public. Fortes differentiates between the domestic and what he calls the "politico-jural" aspects of kinship (Fortes 1969: 73), seeing them as analytically distinct: "Thus, if we take . . . a person's total field of kinship relations, we find that its management involves compliance with norms that emanate from two distinct and in some ways opposed domains of social structure" (Fortes 1969:98). Those opposed domains are the domestic and the politico-jural. The domestic for Fortes is based on the mother-child relationship, which everywhere results in "self-sacrificing love and support on the one side, and lifelong trust and devotion on the other" (Fortes 1969:191). For Fortes, the domestic group "naturally" promotes norms based on "conscience," while norms for public life are based on politico-jural laws (Fortes 1969:191). The latter are political, public, and social, while the former are presocial and affective. Fortes then focuses analytic attention on politico-jural norms and relations since, for him, domestic relations do not vary significantly cross-culturally. Although Fortes asserts a link of some kind between the two domains, he concentrates his investigation on the "public" aspects of kinship. He does not explore the connection.

This brief exploration of some influential social theorists and anthropologists shows that connections between public life and private life have not been the focus of investigation, as they are in this study. Instead, there has been a long tradition of drawing a strict analytical dichotomy between public life and private life. This distinction does not match everyday life and experience in Ireland, as will be shown. The dichotomy also seems to be based on first principles about the nature of private life and public life which may not be entirely useful in this study. I offer some alternate parameters of public life and private life next.

PRIVATE AND PUBLIC RELATIONSHIPS: EMPIRICAL FRAMEWORKS

Private life usually means family life; everything outside the family is public (Morgan 1975:4; Cootnz 1992:125). Some feminist scholars claim that the personal is political, thus demonstrating, they say, that public and private are intertwined (see below). But they equate private life with family life and public life with work or politics, identifying public life as more valuable than private life and leaving the strict dichotomy in place. However, social life is more complex than that.

Delineations of private and public relationships are necessary in order to analyze everyday interactions. Private life consists of more than family life, although it can include, and very often does include, familial relations. Private life consists of *relationships* that are more or less ongoing, continual, and characterized by generalized reciprocity and multiplexity (Swartz 1991:149).[1] Despite cross-cultural variation, private life does seem to involve an emotional intensity that blends with elements of cultural understandings regarding public relationships until interactions take place in anonymous public life. This type of completely public relationship is marked by extremely simplex relationships. Therefore, public life and private life cannot be seen as marked solely by physical space—that is, houses, factories, offices, and so forth are not in themselves public or private. Neither can we say that institutions by themselves, such as bureaucracies, government, corporations, or the state, constitute the public. It is the interaction within these spaces that strongly shapes a person's understanding of space as public or private.

To understand how people blend aspects of cultural understandings regarding public and private relations, we need to look at particular social interactions and specific cultural elements: these are statuses and role relationships and the elements which comprise these cultural complexes (Swartz 1991). A status is a culturally constituted social category, consisting of understandings that guide emotion, thought, and behavior by the individual and the interpretation of and response to that behavior by others (Swartz 1991:7–12). Any individual occupies many statuses throughout her life. A role is a subunit of a status, consisting of a specific set of understandings regarding particular behavior. For example, a person may occupy the status of "mother," which contains a number of roles: the mother may behave differently in the "mother-daughter" role than she might in the "mother-teacher" role.

Different subsets of expectations for behavior, thought, and emotion are used by the participants, depending on the role. By using a status-and-role-based model, we can see how statuses, employed in role relationships, mediate public and private. We can identify specific interactions as made up of different combinations of understandings regarding public and private relationships.[2]

We would note, for example, that, cross-culturally, for almost every person, relationships between family members, extended kin, friends, neighbors, workmates, fellow worshipers, and other community members (Bellah et al. 1985) comprise the multiplex end of social life. Salient status expectations are not necessarily limited and specific even in what are normally considered public social arenas; public life does not necessarily or usually only contain simplex relationships (though private life, as noted above, will always contain multiplex ones). Instead, we need to mark out some universal characteristics of private relationships.

Private relationships have several elements.[3] First, a private relationship is marked by exclusivity. In such a relationship, the individuals have some control over the accessibility of information. An interactional partner in a private relationship often has exclusive access to information that the other has disclosed, intentionally or not. Further, most often there is mutuality of disclosure, though the information disclosed by the partners may not be identical or isomorphic.[4] Second, there are boundaries around the relationship that are culturally recognized as valuable and inviolable. Such a socially recognized, bounded relationship also contains an element of commitment, in that it is at least semipermanent or ongoing, marriage being a primary example. That is, a private relationship is understood to be legitimate.[5] Third, understandings surrounding and shaping a person's behavior in a private relationship are flexible and generalized rather than concrete and limited. As noted above, private relationships are marked by generalized reciprocity, so that one person's actions do not have to be immediately and exactly repaid by one's partner, as would be the case in more simplex relationships. The private, then, consists of socially recognized relationships that are more or less ongoing and which contain information, interactions, and behaviors usually inaccessible to those outside the relationship. If a relationship does not contain these elements, it is not a private relationship as I analyze such relationships in this study. (The private would also include the individual unrevealed to anyone—the private self, with attendant conscious and unconscious conflicts, fantasies, thoughts, emotions, and behaviors that no one else witnesses or experiences [Laufer and Wolf 1977:23]. This set of understandings of course is shaped by culture as well.)

Even those interactions which may appear to be private ought not be characterized as such without further analysis. For example, one offers a good deal of what may appear to be private information when taking a personality inventory with a psychologist (Laufer and Wolf 1977:36). Although the *content* of the information offered may be fairly construed as private, the *relationship* is not. The transitory nature of the relationship puts it outside the strictly private as defined here. Similarly, the act of Confession in the Catholic Church requires discussion of personal behavior and thoughts to a priest. While, again, the content of this interaction contains private information, the expectations surrounding the interaction are not private: the penitent does not expect that the confessor will begin confessing his own sins when the penitent has finished. Indeed, the assumed anonymity of the penitent precludes such behavior. Further, this role relationship is not mutually exclusive: while the penitent may have only one confessor, the confessor has many penitents. Neither example meets the criteria for a private relationship.

At the same time, the examples of the psychologist–test taker and confessor–penitent role relationships reveal a complicating factor in understanding the nature of public and private. Although we cannot characterize these interactions as private relationships despite the private content of the interaction, they contain some elements of understandings regarding private relationships. Both the penitent and the test taker provide information about themselves which few if any other people know. These statuses thus have private *elements, aspects,* or *dimensions*, despite the fact that they are not completely or even primarily private relationships. In fact, all statuses and associated role relationships can be analyzed for private elements. Those which have broad, ongoing, and frequent private elements then can be characterized as primarily private. Some statuses and role relationships usually have strong and more private elements, and others have weak and fewer ones. In order to better understand the nature of public and private social relationships, we must identify those private and public elements of the statuses and role relationships being discussed.[6]

We can contrast public elements of relationships with private elements. Public elements consist of specific reciprocity, so that debts and obligations are repaid quickly and equally. Relationships contain specific, fixed, and limited understandings and expectations: they are simplex rather than multiplex (Swartz 1991:149). In simplex relationships, concrete goals and activities dominate.

So in Dublin, for example, the role relationship "bus driver–passenger" is guided by mainly public understandings. In exchange for paying her fare, a passenger expects that the bus driver will follow a predetermined and published route. The passenger expects that the driver will drive the bus more or less according to traffic laws and that he will allow her to disembark when she has provided the appropriate signal (ringing a bell or standing next to the driver's seat). Neither party, further, would expect the other to begin in-depth discussions of marital problems or other, more private concerns. This role relationship therefore has many more public elements than it does private ones. Activities are limited, fixed, and concrete, and goals are very specific.

Therefore, it becomes clear that statuses and role relationships cannot be classified as "private" or "public" without reference to public and private aspects. Any social situation can be analyzed using this model and a characterization of its relative publicness or privateness can be made. The model contains both etic and emic dimensions. The problem of what is public and what is private arises from the scholarly treatment of this issue; etic concerns frame the analytic concern. However, emic definitions of public and private understandings provide a basis for analysis of any particular society. In this study, I discuss the scholarly problem within the context of what the Irish, and specifically the urban Irish, perceive as appropriately public and what is appropriately private. It should be noted, however, that it is likely that there are exceptions I have not anticipated. Generally, however, the model will hold.

Private life, then, does not always stand in opposition to public life. We cannot logically fit workmates, for instance, in our private lives if we operate from a strict dichotomy of private = family, public = work.[7] Most researchers, both in the past and currently, employ strictly dichotomous models of public life and private life, often assigning agency to institutions and relying on power as the only salient social fact. I discuss that literature next.

RESEARCH ON THE FAMILY

Family life has been the focus of many discussions regarding the nature of public life and private life. Family life, as will be seen below, is usually equated with private life, and public concerns tend to be equated with all other parts of life. My approach differs from these analyses.

Earlier Research: The Private Sphere versus the Public Sphere

In addition to seminal work in the social sciences, other commentators discussing the family and kinship usually conceptualized family life as essentially different from social life; kinship relations were judged to be public and not private. This point of view can be found, for instance, in Robin Fox 1983 [1967]; Parsons and Bales 1955; George P.

Murdock 1949; William G. Goode 1970 [1963]; and Elizabeth Bott, 1971 [1957]. Because of the putative mother–child bond or the special emotional nature of the marital and parental relationship, the family was seen as an affective organization rather than an instrumental one. When at home, one loved and was loved, did not work, relaxed, engaged in leisure activities, played with children, and so forth. A person's activities in the home were contrasted with the more impersonal ones in public. For most researchers in the 1940s, 1950s, and 1960s, the home and the nuclear family was, as Christopher Lasch (1977) put it, "the haven in the heartless world."

It is not clear, however, whether family life, either in the Anglo-American experience or cross-culturally, was an escape.[8] Social historian Stephanie Coontz (1992) shows that the middle-class American ideal of a nuclear family consisting of a breadwinner father, a homemaker mother, and two to three children, all living in a suburban single-family house, was realized by only a very small portion of Americans in the twentieth century (also see Segalen 1986). It certainly is not the norm today and does not seem to be a general cross-cultural model either (see, for example, Goode 1970 and Whiting and Edwards 1988). Yet much research seems to be based on the belief that America—and, by conventional extension, the rest of the world—has a "traditional" family form (see Klatch 1987 and Coontz 1992 for examples of various political and religious positions regarding family life in America).

It could be argued that such research—and certainly most current political debate—is based in unexamined assumptions concerning the universal nature of family life and public life. These assumptions could well be located in a researcher's own fundamental notions about family life, based on his experience as a family member himself in his particular society. All researchers come from and, perhaps, have created families. Such a basic and long-term experience may affect dispassionate questioning regarding the nature of family and public life. Conventional child-rearing and economic arrangements may appear biologically based—"natural"—when instead such arrangements should be investigated. Further, researchers are of course historically and socially situated. An understanding of the social times, as well as the nature of intellectual and scientific trends (Kuhn 1962), helps us understand at least some of the assumptions underlying the social scientific study of public and private life so that we can interpret their data and analyses more fruitfully.

Much of current social science research still operates as if the nuclear family is the only nexus of emotional intimacy (Lasch 1977; Cootnz 1992). Some critics of current social science research say that scholars do not discuss how the larger institutions of American life interact with, interfere with, or invade family life (Lasch 1977; Gerstel and Gross 1987; Thorne 1982; Rapp 1982; Zaretsky 1982; Zenner 1980) or how "corporate capitalism" (for example) relies on the oppression of women by demanding that workers be cared for away from work by women. The critics of the "family-as-haven" paradigm, such as Lasch (1977), argue that researchers still conceptualize the family as an isolated, affect-laden center in an otherwise instrumental world. The critics assert that their own research and argumentation demonstrates that, in fact, the instrumental world of the public impinges on emotionally expressive private life to an onerous degree. That is, the critics argue that public and private are intermixed in varying levels of malevolence. They also want to see the family altered in fundamental ways. Critics of this sort generally fall into two categories: the sociological critic, exemplified by Lasch (1977); and feminist analysis (see below). Because these researchers discuss the public/private dichotomy, and are cited often in studies regarding public and private life, a review of their work is salient.

The Invasion of the Family: The Public Takes Over the Private

Christopher Lasch (1977) is a defender of the "traditional" "Western"[9] extended family, and as such he is cited in nearly every study reviewed herein. As a result, his ideas continue to influence analysis of public and private and family studies; they therefore must be discussed. Lasch decries the current structure of the American family, asserting that social workers, social scientists, psychologists, educators, and other instruments of the state invade the family's integrity. Arguing that the only important function of the family—the socialization of children (Lasch 1977:130)—has been effectively removed by "experts" of one kind or another, Lasch would like us to return to the time when fathers, and only fathers, were in charge of families. Instead, it is teachers, social workers, welfare workers, psychologists, and pediatricians who tell parents how to parent.[10] Families do not rely on extended kin for their wisdom any longer. For Lasch, authority is gone, and individual rights come to the fore,[11] destroying the family as an effective social form. He believes that the family in better times was the only socializer of children, that the family was inviolate in the past. Now, Lasch says, the public sphere—government, welfare systems, education—interferes with the private sphere, assuming responsibility for functions the traditional family used to fill on its own. These public bureaucracies make decisions that fathers used to make, and the bureaucracies act with impunity. Lasch examines theories of family life to show the interpenetration of public and private.

It appears, however, that Lasch's understanding of how things used to be, as well as how things are now cross-culturally, may not match other evidence. Historical and cross-cultural research suggests that parents are not always the only agents of enculturation and socialization for their children. For instance, Beatrice Whiting and Carolyn Edwards (1988), in an update of the "Six Cultures" study on child rearing initiated in the 1950s, demonstrate that peers, siblings, adult relatives other than parents, and other, unrelated adults, have a significant part to play in the socialization of children worldwide, whether the children live in middle-class suburban America or rural African societies. Moreover, Nadine Peacock's discussion of Efe family life (1991) shows that villagers share child care, including breast feeding, education, and enculturation, rather than seeing child rearing as the sole responsibility of an isolated nuclear family. Further, Peter Laslett, a family historian, shows that, from at least the seventeenth century, European families either sent their children to serve other families or employed young children as servants (Laslett 1977). It appears that at least 80% of European children were either exposed to child servants or were themselves child servants in the seventeenth and eighteenth centuries (Laslett 1977:43). The young servants, Laslett remarks, were "having an effect on the infant children of" their employers (Laslett 1977:43). Strangers were entering, and presumably affecting, European family life. Evidence from Europe (see also Prost 1991), Africa, and from the Six Cultures study indicates that the family may not have been inviolate historically or cross-culturally (see Coontz 1988 and 1992 for corroborating evidence regarding the history of American family life).

The "family besieged" (the subtitle of Lasch's 1977 work) apparently has no power, ability, willingness, or choice to ignore the intrusiveness of institutions. Eli Zaretsky, in a brief criticism of Lasch (Zaretsky 1982:190), notes that Lasch assumes that all families are equal victims of the onslaught of expertise from the public sphere.[12] However, Zaretsky continues, the families most likely to be invaded by the state—dependent on welfare or with jailed members (that is, mainly poor people)—are not necessarily representative of every American family. Zaretsky points out that "the rest of us" may well be positively affected by therapists, teachers, doctors, and the other experts Lasch condemns (1977). Still, Lasch identifies the cult of the bureaucratic expert as responsible for significantly altering American family life.

The Liberation of Women from Family Work

A large body of sociological, social historical, and anthropological work deals with the interpenetration of public and private. These scholars, who categorize themselves as feminist scholars, analyze the demise of the "traditional" family outlined by Lasch (1977) even as they assert, as Lasch does, that current economic forms (e.g., corporate capitalism, government, or the welfare system) invade private life. Researchers concerned with these ideas try to show that the family is not necessarily the emotional haven from a heartless world of work, thus demonstrating, they say, that public and private intermingle. Also, this set of reformers envisions a world in which unconventional family forms will be accepted, if not celebrated.[13] Single-parent families, gay and lesbian unions, communal living arrangements, dual-job families, blended families, and other nontraditional family organizations are as legitimate, to this group of scholars, as the "monolithic American family of monogamous permanent heterosexual unions with children" (Thorne 1982:2). By rejecting what these researchers see as public, dominant-culture, instrumental, patriarchal, sexist ideology, we will be freed to do what we wish in our private lives without public, moralistic repercussions. In this view, women, especially, will gain more power and authority as a result of drastically altering family structure. As will be seen, however, much of this work assumes, like earlier researchers discussed above, that there are two separate social domains, with two completely different sets of expectations and behaviors. The research is largely theoretical and seems based in first principles regarding patriarchy and the oppression of women, which are presented as self-evident rather than being proven.

The public world of work, politics, and economic activity is valued by this group of researchers, who see family life as a powerless sphere and entirely oppressive to women (for example, Gerstel and Gross 1987; Rosaldo 1974, 1980). What these researchers see as "public life" is instrumental and rational, and power, the salient variable for the analysis, is unfairly distributed so that only men have effective access to it. Family life, on the other hand, for which women are solely and unfairly responsible, contains no useful power and consists only of a distracting ideology of love; analysts argue that this is wrong and must be changed so that women have power in the public sphere. It is unclear what will then happen to family life. These researchers rely on a clear distinction between public and private life (see Strathern 1984), but they also assert that public and private are intertwined.

This set of analyses argues that the "traditional," "privatized" nuclear family, as well as corporate capitalism, relies upon women's unpaid work in the home, robbing women of economic, political, and social ("public") power. Women, in this view, should have the right to participate in waged labor rather than unpaid housework (Thorne 1982:2; Sacks 1984a:2). In order to liberate women from the drudgery of housework and child care, feminist analysts argue that a radical reformation of family and capitalist life must occur.

Work and private (family) life are so intertwined, say these researchers, that the public influences the private egregiously. Through general discussions of wage labor and corporate capitalism (Thorne 1982; Sacks 1984a:2), the family as a center of unequal power and labor (for example, Rapp 1982; Ferree 1984; Sacks 1984b; Gerstel and Gross 1987), "macrosociological" analyses (Gerstel and Gross 1987:1), and the overall ideologically and actually subordinate positions in which women are placed in the family and in general universally (Rosaldo 1974, 1980; Yanagisako 1977:189), these analysts argue that it is obvious that public and private are intrinsically interwoven. Oppressed with an ideology of altruism, love, and sacrifice in the service of the family (Gerstel and Gross 1987:3–4), they say that women do unpaid work in the home, cooking, cleaning, washing, ironing, and caring for children. This is *work*, identified by the researchers as a public activity. It should not be understood as "private" simply because it takes place in the home or seems motivated by "love." Further, this work is crucial to family existence (Sacks 1984b). That women perform this work is important, say these analysts.

Feminist analysts also argue that women's position in the family renders them publicly and privately powerless despite the very real work they do. These writers wish to overturn conventional understandings regarding women's work and radically alter the family so that women, as well as men, have opportunities to work, for wages, outside the home. Their analyses center on identifying how women's work for the family is crucially similar to more public, powerful forms of work but is not rewarded by the conferring of power.[14] Again, this is primarily a theoretical, rather than an empirically based, argument.

Power is the key analytic concept employed in this branch of family analysts. Concern here is with the acquisition—if not appropriation—of legitimate political, economic, public authority by, presumably, all women. Men, in this conceptualization, are rarely discussed. The many strands that draw men and women together and those which keep them together are either wholly absent or reconfigured as tools of a capitalist economy (Rapp 1982). So, for example, needs for nurturance, affection, and love are not addressed. For these researchers, power is the only motivation behind social life, more insidious since it is hidden. Love and altruism are presented in this literature as ideologies built with the tools of the patriarchy (Rapp 1982). These authors value instrumentality over affective relations in their work. They seem to accept the dichotomy of public and private as well, although they assert otherwise.

Feminist researchers look at the interpenetration of public and private in several ways. First, women's unequal position is due to their powerless residence in the domestic arena (Rosaldo 1974, 1980), a re-

sult of a surfeit of power held by men in the public sphere. Power relations in the public sphere shape, if not determine, relations in the
private sphere. Second, because women do real, important work in the
family home, the public (work) and the private (the family home) are
blended. Finally, agency is assigned to institutions—capitalism, patriarchy, the state—over which women have no influence.

However, these positions rely on a distinction between public and
private different from that which I offer. In these analyses, women's
work in the home is held up to an imagined instrumental standard of
work in the public sphere and is assessed to be similarly experienced
and motivated. A concept of "real" work in the public sphere, in this
instance, is assumed to be the salient comparative unit by these researchers. Work done in the home is not held to be the standard against
which public work should be judged; the noninstrumental aspects of
the public life of work are not addressed. It is a public definition that
is used to appraise private activities. When public and private truly
intermingle, noninstrumental motivations that obtain in the various
public and private spheres in which humans interact can be seen (see
discussion regarding work relationships below).

Much of this work is theoretical rather than data based. It appears
that analysts here do not identify the social mechanisms by which the
"state" or the "patriarchy" create oppressive structures. Assigning motivation and agency beyond the individual may not be the most effective
way to understand publicness and privateness. A family is not an agent,
as Naomi Gerstel and Harriet Gross (1987:1) argue it is. It is a small
group with specific interplaying dynamics (compare Minuchin 1974;
Haley 1980; Madanes 1981). But those dynamics are initiated, enacted,
and experienced by individuals in specific statuses and role relationships.

Finally, it is not necessarily so that all behavior at work, or other
more or less public arenas, is motivated solely by power needs, just as
all behavior in the family is not solely motivated by nurturance needs.
When we demonstrate the similarities, not just the differences, in public and private understandings, expectations, and behaviors across a
wide range of variables, we will have seen the continuities that link
public and private in immediate and identifiable ways. We will further
be able to understand the continuities as well as the differences of public and private life cross-culturally as we see human behavior in moti-
vational complexity.

WORK AND FAMILY LIFE

One way to understand the complexities of work and family life is to
examine the multiple motivations and different sorts of role relationships operating in both. Anthropologists and sociologists, such as Kath-

ryn Dudley (1994), Sandra Cullen (1994), Rosemary Pringle (1994), Karen Sacks (1984c), and Arlie Hochschild (1983, 1989, 1997), have studied various work environments, and their data regarding work experiences clearly shows that power is not the sole motivator for most workers. Instead, workers gain and maintain a positive sense of identity and contribution, and they form friendships with coworkers—a case of an activity, work, conventionally placed in the public sphere, influencing the actions in private life and vice versa in a continual loop (Dudley 1994). Other workers find that the basic performance of their jobs requires the use of aspects of private concerns and statuses in their work (Cullen 1994). The very nature of secretarial work requires a deeply personal relationship with one's boss; an apparently public social arena demands a typically private role relationship (Pringle 1994 following Kanter 1977). And others might adopt understandings and behavioral patterns from private life—family statuses and role relationships—in the workplace (Sacks 1984c). Currently, employees in many workplaces find work to be the "haven" and family experiences—the private—to be the "heartless world" (Hochschild 1989, 1997). Recent scholarship shows that work—one aspect of the public—is not necessarily the heartless world which stands in opposition to the comfort of the family.

Dudley (1994) studied the social effects of the closing of an auto factory in Kenosha, Wisconsin. In discussing their factory experience, informants make it clear that they did not view themselves as automatons, alienated in the Marxist sense, with no identity and with only instrumental motivations in their work life. Dudley talks with "Luis," a third-generation Chicano who had worked at the auto plant for a number of years before it closed (Dudley 1994:45–46). Luis speaks of his factory work with warmth and commitment; it was not necessarily an alienating experience (compare Clayre 1974:223). Luis enjoyed working at the plant and found a sense of himself through his work; this came from doing a job that was recognized by co-workers and others in the marketplace as valuable. Dudley analyzes further: "Work has meaning because it is truly one of the few ways in American society that people can demonstrate their moral worth. Every occupation provides a stage on which our moral character can be displayed, and an attentive audience from whom we seek validation and applause" (Dudley 1994:45–46). Luis saw auto work as an integral part of who he was, including him in a moral community, making him an adult, bringing him friends as well as material goods. He ends by assessing auto work: " 'It's been me' " (Dudley 1994:46). Luis's understanding of his work is wrapped up inextricably with his sense of himself: the public world of work has shaped, in a positive way from Luis's perspective, the private sense of identity.

Dudley goes on to discuss the formation of informal groups on the assembly line that act to protect and shield workers when one is having a bad day. Friendship, solidarity, understanding all operate to nurture workers who are not performing as well as they could. Multiplex relationships are evident in a public arena in which we would think only simplex ones would exist if we accepted the simple public/private dichotomy. Dudley tells us that workers will take up others' slack in a form of generalized reciprocity: "This system of exchange links workers into a network of informal obligations that compel future reciprocity of action and collective responsibility. For although group assistance is more or less freely given, it is always extended with the vague but implicit expectation that the favor will be returned someday, whenever the recipient is able to do so" (Dudley 1994:114). Rather than operating from purely instrumental motives within simplex relationships, the auto workers in Kenosha relied on more multiplex understandings. Reciprocity was general, not specific; timing of reciprocity was vague, not specified. Here again we see the intermingling of private multiplex relationships and public work.

Other researchers have shown that a worker's social placement in neighborhoods and towns influences work performance. Cullen (1994) discusses English welfare and benefits workers in smaller towns, describing a prestige hierarchy of job placement workers at the top, unemployment benefits workers below them, and welfare service workers at the bottom. She notes that all the workers lived in the area; they were not viewed, by themselves or by their neighbors, as an elite managerial class but rather were seen as clerks. Cullen looks at how private and public concerns meet, particularly with regard to unemployment workers (who decide who can receive benefits):

> A majority of staff had personal experience of unemployment, at least for a short time, and were aware that ultimately they might have had need of welfare benefits themselves. Thus personal and professional interests coincided. Staff protected "the system" for the "deserving" clients, which potentially included themselves and their families, and sought to save "the system" from the "undeserving" clients who were believed to be undermining it. (citation omitted) (Cullen 1994:144)

Instead of a rational, instrumental workplace bureaucracy in which workers rigidly apply rules regardless of personal interest, we see welfare and benefits workers bringing personal, family and private concerns into the workplace (see also Prost 1991:116). This demonstrates the intermingling and continuous nature of public and private activities. More than one status—welfare worker—operates in this situation; family member, potentially unemployed person, morally correct person are all present as well. Through an analysis of different statuses and their saliences, it becomes clear that public work is not always or merely about instrumental behavior or rational bureaucracy (it should be noted that neither Cullen nor Dudley—nor the other researchers discussed below—analyze their data in terms of statuses, role relationships, cultural understandings, or different kinds of expectations, identifiers, or saliences). Cullen's data show that work and private concerns are tied up very closely indeed.

Pringle (1994) investigates expectations and behavior surrounding the status secretary. Updating Kanter's (1977) characterization of secretarial work as one requiring personal loyalty and commitment to the boss (Kanter 1977:69, 82), Pringle analyzes the personal nature of the role relationship (boss–secretary) along sexual lines, saying that the role relationship "is organized around sexuality and family imagery" (Pringle 1994:117). She goes on to assert, based on her fieldwork in an English corporation, that "the relationship is based on personal rapport and involves a degree of intimacy and shared secrets unusual for any but lovers or close friends. It is capable of generating intense feelings of loyalty, dependency, and personal commitment" (Pringle 1994:117). Belying the Weberian "ideal type" of bureaucracy as rational and instrumental, the boss–secretary role relationship in a modern corporation—the public—is based on personal, private expectations. The public and the private here blend.

Sacks (1984c) provides another instance of the complex interpenetration of public and private understandings at work. Although, like the other researchers discussed above, Sacks does not analyze her data in this way, her study of ward secretaries shows the application of private, family statuses and understandings to the work environment of a southern U.S. hospital (see also Zenner 1980:137–142). Sacks's analysis centers on metaphors and values rather than behavior: "Ward secretaries discussed the good hospital worker in many of the same ways that they discussed the good adult in a family. Their rules of behavior at work were expressed in family terms and concepts. This suggests that family relationships are an important source for practical meanings of adulthood, autonomy, hierarchy, and equality" (Sacks 1984c: 284). Note that Sacks is discussing meanings and rules rather than actual behavior; nonetheless, it appears that ward secretaries applied their understandings regarding family statuses and role relationships at work.

Sacks also goes into some detail about the formation of friendship. Her informants discuss the importance of friendship, stating that friends are much more reliable for emotional and practical assistance than family (Sacks 1984c:285). Here we see the complexity of the aspects of public and private understandings, however briefly. Relationships begun in the public sphere of work take on private aspects yet are not family relationships; in fact, friendships are contrasted favorably with family relationships (Sacks 1984c:285). Close friendships challenge the simple dichotomy of public and private, as Sacks's data so clearly indicate.[15]

Finally, Arlie Hochschild's continuing project (1983, 1989, 1997) on the interplay between American family life and work illustrates the interpenetration of public and private arenas. Using ethnographic methods in her sociological studies, Hochschild describes, variously, the corporate appropriation of what conventionally is seen as "private" emotional expression and experience (Hochschild 1983), the conflict working women face between workplace and family demands (Hochschild 1989), and the tension both fathers and mothers experience as they attempt to commit fully both to their employers and their families (Hochschild 1997). In all three instances, Hochschild asserts that capitalism and the workplace win hands down, providing emotional intimacy, enduring friendships, fulfillment, and the "haven" in ways the family no longer does (if it ever did) (Hochschild 1997).

Recent research regarding the experience of work demonstrates, then, that a division between public and private may not fit with everyday life. Work is not necessarily a solely instrumental, alienating, and rational activity. Instead, workers find ways to bring themselves, their understandings and expectations regarding human interaction, and, in some ways, their families, into work. Intimate friendships, collegial relationships, kindnesses, loyalty, and help frequently are part and parcel of work relationships, just as they are meant to be for family relationships. Given that this is so, it may be in order to revise scholarly analysis regarding a stark split between public life and private life.

PUBLIC LIFE AND PRIVATE RELATIONSHIPS

Public and private elements blend to guide behavior in statuses and role relationships; public and private do not comprise only a simple dichotomy. We do not live either in havens or heartless worlds; rather, social life is much more complex. Specifically, private life has components that can be identified; if an interaction is analyzed that does not contain any of these elements, it is very likely not private. We examined early social theory and saw that seminal scholars have asserted or assumed that a strict dichotomy between public life and private life exists. Next, research conceptualizing families as havens was discussed; Christopher Lasch served as exemplar. The largely theoretical feminist discussions of the family were next described. Detailed ethnographies of work were then examined, the data from which clearly show that the workplace does not comport with a picture of a cold, heartless world.

Rather, it can often be a social arena of emotional support, generalized reciprocity, multiplex relationships, and complex and shifting statuses and role relationships, sometimes in contrast to home life.

Later chapters discuss Irish familial statuses and associated role relationships, using an analysis of the elements of public and private understandings guiding some behaviors in contemporary Dublin. First, however, in Chapter 2, I provide a history of Ireland, with special attention paid to the interaction of public life, private life, the Catholic Church, and British colonialism. Chapter 3 presents a general overview of Irish cultural understandings. Chapter 4 focuses specifically on Dublin. Chapter 5 presents a general outline of the blending of public and private understandings in Dublin, discussing several different cases. Chapters 6, 7, and 8 analyze Irish understandings, experiences, and behaviors regarding motherhood, fatherhood, and marital life, respectively, pinpointing some statuses and role relationships for the blend of public and private elements. Chapter 9 provides summaries and conclusions regarding Irish family life and the nature of the analysis of public and private elements in Ireland, in social science, and in American politics.

NOTES

1. Recall that multiplex relationships are marked by general expectations for thought, feelings, and behavior on the part of participants in the relationship. Swartz remarks: "The expectations in multiplex relationships cross a number of cultural domains and are usually broad and general rather than specific and concrete" (Swartz 1991:149). Simplex relationships, on the other hand, involve very limited and defined expectations.

2. See Medick and Sabean (1984) for a somewhat similar but less specific argument.

3. Margulis (1977), a social psychologist, identifies some of the elements discussed here.

4. For example, a wife may discuss her feelings about a neighbor's behavior while her husband may discuss his day at work. The point is not that the content of discussions or interactions is identical, but rather that some sort of discussion takes place in which others outside the relationship do not share. It is the continual and frequent *process* of interaction within the context of exclusivity and multiplexity that is key here.

5. This is contrasted with secret behavior, which consists of interactions, behaviors, and thoughts that are negatively valued by society and, perhaps, by the individual (Warren and Laslett 1977:44). Secret behavior is hidden from view, primarily because it would be punished if others knew about it. Private behavior, on the other hand, is recognized as legitimately kept away from others.

6. I use "aspects," "elements," or "dimensions" interchangeably throughout this study. The terms are imprecise but refer to subsets of cultural understand-

ings and the expectations held by parties to an interaction regarding cognitive-emotional state and behaviors. Each participant in a role relationship will have a general cultural guide concerning the appropriate use of understandings concerning what is public and what is private. That general guide is honed and modified by specific situations and interactions. Role relationships influence behavior, thought, and emotion in real space and time; they are not static and unchanging. As a result, using my model, it is not possible to specifically predict the individual subsets of understandings which a person will use in her interactions. However, the model makes analysis of observed interactions more accurate and flexible than the use of a model based on a strictly dichotomous view of public and private social arenas.

7. Throughout this book, I employ the conventional dichotomous terminology of "public" and "private" even as I argue that it is more sensible to soften the dichotomy. The shorthand terms of "public" and "private" are almost unavoidable. There are, indeed, sets of understandings that are used in "private" relationships, as argued above. There are also more "public" understandings. However, relationships should be analyzed for public and private aspects before being classified, rather than being characterized as belonging solely to either public or private life. Until we take the complexity of these sets of relationships into account, we will continue to see public and private dichotomously (see also Vincent 1991).

8. Margery Wolf's studies of Taiwanese families (1968, 1972), for instance, quite clearly showed that family life—at least for newly married women—was work and almost totally work. The home was not a comforting haven for the young Taiwanese women with whom Wolf talked (although women's social position changed through time, so that older women had more prestige and less work than did younger women).

9. When Lasch speaks of Western families or a Western marital pattern (Lasch 1977:5), he apparently means "American." Lasch does not define which West he means, and he provides no proof that there is a unified Western family structure or marital pattern. The equation of so-called Western values, understandings, and behaviors with English and American ones is a troublesome practice. Data from Ireland indicate that, while some patterns are shared between the Irish, the English, and Americans, many others are not. The West is a term bandied about with no little carelessness; yet it is not at all clear that the West consists of one set of cultural understandings. See Ouroussoff (1993) for an extended discussion.

10. There is a much smaller body of sociological work that, like Lasch, deals with the way we "used to be." Bensman and Lilienfeld (1979) serve as exemplars. They argue that the modern corporation has created a split between public and private domains for the individual, in that instrumentality is valued and intimacy is not (Bensman and Lilienfeld 1979:44–45). They further assert that, in "primitive" [*sic*] societies, a person has many "warm communal primary roles" that allow more authenticity and completeness (Bensman and Lilienfeld 1979:15; see also Moore 1984). Empirical evidence is not provided. However, in many simpler societies, statuses and role relationships can be marked by complexity, lack of intimacy and warmth, and a rigidity with which statuses and

role relationships are frequently imbued. See Reiter 1975 for a similar argument.

11. See Sennett (1977) for a similar argument.

12. Sweden's extensive government network of social services is discussed in a manner more sympathetic than Lasch's in Orfali (1991).

13. Shere Hite, in a June 1995 interview on National Public Radio, discussed the "democratization of the family" and exhorted us to found our families on love and feelings rather than duty, commitment, and traditional gender statuses. Only by doing so will we rid ourselves of the insidious sexism that still rules "traditional" family life, since women, according to Hite, are entirely responsible for the success of families.

14. There is a body of work that argues the opposite. In societies where there is strict separation of the sexes, women typically have control over the household or control emotional resources otherwise unavailable to their men. Some researchers claim that women have a good deal of power as a result of what appears to be a clear dichotomy of public and private. Even in those societies which allow women little extradomestic legitimate authority, their influence can be extraordinary. This is particularly so when women use their status as "mother" as entry into political battles (see, for example, Rogers 1975; Reiter 1975; Molnar 1982; Nelson 1974; Susser 1986; Swartz 1982).

15. There seems to be little scholarly work discussing how friendship fits into public life and private life in different societies. Brain (1976) deals with the subject of friendship in different societies but does not discuss public and private specifically in this context.

CHAPTER 2

Politics, the Church, and Authority

Patterns of authority in the Catholic Church and former occupying forces of the English continue to influence Irish cultural understandings. This can be seen in the expression and experience of the blending of public and private understandings in 1990s Dublin relationships. In this chapter, I will explore contemporary Irish historical and social scientific studies, presenting a picture of Ireland as it has been understood by Irish scholars.[1] Further I enlarge the discussion with some historical facts generally not mentioned in the history presented by informants. For many Irish people—urban, town, or rural—a highly centralized authority structure (whether it be the Church or the Irish State) remains today in postcolonial Ireland. Chapter 8 will demonstrate how this cultural complex of understandings concerning unquestioned and unquestionable authority and associated understandings is associated with understandings concerning appropriate emotional and corporeal experience and expression. Here, however, I provide a rudimentary sketch of Irish history as my informants apparently understand it, and as Irish scholars expand upon everyday Irish knowledge; the two generally, though not always (as will be seen), match in general outline. I also discuss present-day governmental and religious organization and

experience and their connections with Irish understandings of what is
public and what is private.

The Church's influence on Irish men and women as well as on legislation and public policy makes Ireland a particularly interesting case
with regard to the analysis of the blend of public and private elements
in interaction. The Catholic Church has been important in Irish culture, shaping understandings[2] as well as state policy regarding behavior that has been understood in social science as "private"—family life,
sexual morality, and personal medical care (see discussion of the
Mother and Child Scheme below). In Western Europe, as in the United
States, religion largely has been "privatized," in that religious practice
does not permeate everyday life. Most Western Europeans, and certainly many Americans, consider spirituality to be an individual, "personal" matter (Bellah et al. 1985:224); we see this in the clear (but
currently contested) separation of "church" and "state" in North America. In Ireland, however, the Catholic Church has worked actively in
many aspects of Irish social life, and, as is not the case with many other
Western nations, Irish adherence to the faith remains remarkably
strong in the face of modernization (Hornsby-Smith and Whelan 1994:
22–23).

As will be seen, current Church and governmental organizations, in
part, reflect and shape Irish understandings about what is private and
what is public. A centralized and authoritarian power structure in both
organizations influence the arenas in which the Irish expression of independence and challenges to established authority is considered appropriate. Church doctrine in Ireland, despite relative relaxation of
some Catholic rules after Vatican II, remains generally unquestioned
(Dillon 1993:108–109; Hornsby-Smith and Whelan 1994:16–18); furthermore, a priest friend commented that in general the clergy, and
specifically his bishop, strongly frown upon any challenge to their authority. Since, as Chapter 8 demonstrates, the Catholic Church has
instructed its Irish flock, implicitly in more recent years and explicitly
before 1980 or so, that expression of emotion and physical pleasure is
sinful, and because the Church actively discourages attempts to question that dictate, we can see that the history and structure of the Irish
Catholic Church can be important in understanding its influence on
Irish cultural understandings despite changes in the position of the
Catholic Church in deciding legislative issues. The Hierarchy, as will
be seen, until very recently had defined sexual behavior, child rearing,
reproductive control, marital relationships, and the structure and specific practice of religious belief as under its control.[3] In other words,
what most other Westerners, as well as social scientists, consider to be
private matters instead have been defined by Church authorities as
matters open to extrafamilial clerical scrutiny; Irish sociologist Mi-

chelle Dillon remarks that "the boundaries between public and private morality were formally blurred by" the Church's influence on public policy (Dillon 1993:23). The Irish Hierarchy has regarded governmental officials as incompetent to direct public policy until very recently, insisting that Catholic doctrine should guide all legislation. The cultural complex of understandings pertaining to what is perceived to be public and what is perceived to be private, including family, work, and political behavior and experience, fits well within Hierarchy dictates, although, again, this complex is changing rapidly. Nonetheless, the Church, political organization, Irish history, role relationships in the family, and understandings regarding emotional and physical expression and experience are all connected and support each other. Ireland is an appropriate case to demonstrate how public life and private life blend in complicated and nondichotomous ways as a result.

Furthermore, Irish political clientism (Komito 1994), discussed below, discourages active political activity on the part of constituents. Instead, a friendly but supplicant relationship with one's political representative is the primary guarantee that a constituent's political needs will be met. The political representative will mediate between the constituent and the power broker, much as the priest mediates between an individual Catholic and God. Like Church role relationships, political role relationships have an asymmetrical authoritarian nature. Public activity and relationships, then, are influenced by Irish political organization, and Irish definitions of privacy are expanded with Church intervention. What the Irish discern as "public" and "private" concerns are shaped, in part, by political and religious authority structures.[4] Later chapters discussing Irish mothers and fathers show how Dubliners use their understandings regarding what is public and what is private as they blend these dimensions in different role relationships. Here, however, Irish history as Irish scholars and Irish people generally know it is presented.

The "ethnographic present" is 1995.

A BRIEF HISTORY OF IRELAND

The history my informants and Irish scholars discussed has two main themes. There is what they see as brutal domination by the English.[5] Standing almost in opposition is the influence of the Catholic Church and its unwavering interest in family life and individual behaviors. While informants castigate English treatment of the Irish, they do not seem as concerned with the influence of the Church on their lives. The Catholic Church has had, however, a long-standing influence on Irish cultural understandings regarding what the Church considers its business. As will be shown in later chapters, individual thought, emotion, and behavior are considered by the Church to be under its supervision (Winter 1973; Browne 1986). At the same time, the Irish are extraordinarily devout and have relied on the Church for emotional, physical, and educational sustenance and protection for many centuries.

Prehistory

Ireland's history, like the history of almost any people, involves domination by outside forces, though its prehistory is more difficult to characterize. It appears, from the archaeological sites scattered throughout the island, that humans have inhabited Ireland from at least 5000 B.C. and very likely earlier than that (Corish 1985:1–4). Partly on the basis of linguistic similarities between Irish, Welsh, and Breton, all of which are Celtic languages, scholars judge it likely that a limited number of settlers arrived from both the northwest coast of France and from England some time during the eighth and sixth centuries B.C. (Corish 1985). The Romans never ventured to Ireland, remaining only in England. Ireland, then, was more or less insular until the return of St. Patrick the Briton in the fifth century A.D. (Corish 1985).

Catholicism

Patrick came back to Ireland from England, after escaping slavery as a shepherd there, with the intention of converting the Irish to Catholicism (Cahill 1995:101–115). Although he probably did not drive out all the snakes and convert the entire island, as popular myth has it, it is likely that Patrick was an important evangelical force. He *did* introduce Catholicism to a number of Irish, most notably in the north and west of the island, where most of the holy sites associated with Patrick are located and still venerated (Cahill 1995:115–116; Taylor 1995; Inglis 1987:21). The Church remained, and grew, even after Patrick's death and even with a drastically politically divided island.

At the time of Patrick's arrival, Ireland was parceled into a number of kingdoms. Oftentimes these kingdoms were at war with each other over land and peasant loyalties. The growth of the Catholic Church in premedieval Ireland added another potent ingredient to the kingdoms' brew as clerics vied for power in often-violent clashes over the various kings' subjects (Corish 1985:13). Priests, archbishops, cardinals, and, ultimately, popes appear to have gained significant influence over commoners by the twelfth century (Corish 1985). In addition to the Church's victories in military arenas, clerical influence spread, in part, because of a widespread feeling that Ireland was a uniquely civilized Catholic nation in the midst of European medieval corruption, decay, and immorality (Dillon 1993:12; Cahill 1995).

The Church and British Colonialism

To solidify its military and political influence, the Catholic Church requested the "civilizing" influence of the English, who were still Catholic in the twelfth century. In 1155, Pope Adrian authorized Henry II to occupy Ireland in the service of the Church (Johnson 1980:16). Henry, however, was never particularly interested in Ireland, and by 1175 the English had begun "the tragic English tradition of benign (some would say malign) neglect" of Ireland (Johnson 1980:19).[6]

Irish kings and lords were quick to seize upon English interest—or lack of it—in Ireland and jockeyed for position with English monarchs for the next few centuries. By the thirteenth century, there was occasional English occupation of Ireland, primarily in Dublin and surrounding areas and coastal towns (Johnson 1980:20). The interior still was being fought over, for the most part, by Irish kings and lords (that interior is described at length in Patterson 1994). At the same time, the Church in Ireland continued to encourage English intervention in Ireland, seemingly to counter Irish kings' power, paganism, and blatant disregard for the Church (Johnson 1980:20–21).

The clash between the Church and Irish kings led, in large part, to a growing English presence in Ireland. On the one hand, the Church asked for English help: the Archbishop of Cashel successfully petitioned Edward I to decree that English law, rather than what was seen by the Church as Irish pagan law (the more egalitarian Brehon tradition), applied to all Irish people (Johnson 1980:21). On the other hand, Irish kings asked Scots warriors to assist in battles between the various Irish kingdoms; as a result, a number of Scots settled in Ulster in the latter half of the 1200s (Johnson 1980:22). It is more than a little ironic that two of the more emotional truths for 1990s Ireland—the Catholic Church as being a peculiarly Irish (and thus nationalist) institution and Ulster as having been invaded by the English—are in historical fact inverted. That is, the Catholic Church requested English colonial intervention, and Irish kings, in service of their own aims, invited the ancestors of current-day Ulster residents to stay. Unlike colonial actions by European powers in other arenas—Africa, Asia, and the Americas—the English did not explore, "discover," and ultimately impose themselves on the Irish: they were invited in by the apparent defender of the Irish, the Catholic Church.[7] No informants included this information in their histories of Ireland.

The Growth of English Power

English occupation, always somewhat grudging, grew slowly through the Middle Ages. The English became concerned about the assimilation of Irish ways by English settlers. The Irish parliament, consisting of

Anglo-Irish landholders, passed what were basically miscegenation laws. This established in effect the Dublin Pale, an area in and around Dublin beyond which no English person should go (Johnson 1980:24–25).

The rejection of Catholicism by Henry VIII eventually led to English discrimination against Irish Catholics. Catholics in Ireland were not allowed to own arable land without taking the Protestant Oath of Supremacy. At the same time, most Irish Catholics were not allowed to take the Oath and were, in effect, dispossessed of their lands in favor of either English or Anglo-Irish settlers (Johnson 1980:41; Dillon 1993: 12–13). Finally, the various settlement, or "plantation," decrees ceded huge tracts of land to Scots and English settlers in Ulster; Johnson says that "by the end of the 1630s, in six Ulster counties, Protestants owned 3,000,000 of 3,500,000 acres" (Johnson 1980:42). In addition, in other parts of Ireland, the Irish were forced to leave their lands as the English put together plantations for a favored few (Johnson 1980).

The seventeenth century also saw the arrival of Oliver Cromwell to Ireland's shores, appointed by Charles I to be Lord Lieutenant and General (Johnson 1980:49). Cromwell set about conquering the entire island in the name of England, altering the course of benign neglect England had shown thus far.[8] He was largely successful in his eradication campaign (Johnson 1980:53). Driven by an apparent need to suppress, if not obliterate, all Catholicism in Ireland, Cromwell and his followers forcibly and often violently removed Catholics from land previously recognized by the British Crown as belonging to the Irish (Johnson 1980:57). Protestants increased their ownership of Irish land from 41% in the 1640s to 78% by 1670 (Johnson 1980:57).

By 1700, the English had a firm grip on Ireland, despite abortive attempts at rebellion by the Irish (assisted by the French). The English tightened the grip, promulgating harsher and harsher laws—the "penal laws"—regulating the livelihoods and religious practices of the native Irish (Johnson 1980:61). Most of the laws were directed at first toward the Irish Catholic middle class, rather than the landless and poverty-stricken peasants. The penal laws dealt primarily with the practice of Catholicism as well as with land ownership and the practice of certain professions. Specifically, the penal laws imposed by the British government "prohibited the administering of the sacraments, terminated Catholic education, including the education and ordination of priests, and ordered the exiling of priests and bishops"; these laws were aimed at eradicating the Catholic Church in Ireland (Dillon 1993:13).

However, the laws were more or less ineffective: priests were trained in Europe—primarily in France—and Catholics found ways to practice their religion regardless (Dillon 1993:13). My late mother, with three of her four grandparents fully Irish, frequently told a family legend that demonstrates the unwavering Irish adherence to Catholicism. My mother's great-great-grandfather in County Galway had such a strong faith, or so it was said, that he disobeyed the penal laws by organizing Masses to be said in hedgerows and trees; nothing could keep him from practicing his faith, not even the English. That Irish immigrants to the United States carried tales of secret defiance of the despised penal laws indicates both the ineffectiveness of the penal laws and a clear hatred of the English. Moreover, Johnson notes that the penal laws influenced Irish culture significantly: "Ireland became a country where privilege was upheld, and revenge planned, by the swearing of oaths. Catholic oaths were secret and furtive. Protestant oaths were public and assertive,[9] indeed vainglorious and provocative, being turned into toasts" (Johnson 1980:63). This legacy of colonialism, then, in which Catholicism was repressed and punished and Protestantism was celebrated and rewarded, saw its zenith under Cromwellians in the eighteenth century. In actual fact, however, it was likely not only Catholicism and Irishness that were penalized; as the century wore on, it was the *Catholic Irish peasantry* that suffered the most. The Catholic poor were the colonial targets. Ironically, the penal laws strengthened the Catholic peasantry; they "contributed to the consolidation of the Catholic church and Irish Catholic identity," so that Catholicism provided the Irish with an opportunity to maintain a national identity distinct from the English and the Anglo-Irish Ascendancy (Dillon 1993:14).

Despite the establishment of a uniquely Irish Catholic identity, the Anglo-Irish Ascendancy—the Protestant landowners who were, nonetheless, considered by the English government to be much more Irish than English given their families' long-standing occupation of Irish lands—suffered as well. The eighteenth and nineteenth centuries saw the rise of a dissatisfied Ascendancy. Finding themselves increasingly impoverished by the financial demands of the English Crown, appalled, at least to a degree, by the desperate poverty of the Irish peasantry, and inspired in part by the successful American revolution, the largely Protestant members of the Irish parliament began agitating for, at the very least, Home Rule (Johnson 1980:65–75). They were not successful, despite the efforts of various English and Anglo-Irish reformers and the occasional uprising by the Irish peasantry (Johnson 1980:75–86).

Home Rule did not become a real possibility until the 1830s, when the "Great Emancipator," Daniel O'Connell, rose to political prominence. Supported by Anglo-Irish and the peasantry alike, O'Connell inspired a growing violent Catholic movement. This movement, eventually to become the Irish Republican Army, was stymied by the Great Famine (1843–1851), as was O'Connell. The crisis of the famine hushed the cries for independence (Johnson 1980:91–100).

The Great Hunger

The Irish economy, with the exception of the industrialized Ulster towns of Derry and Belfast (Curtin et al. 1994:2), was overwhelmingly dependent on agriculture as a sole source of income for most Irish people. The widespread failure of the potato crops and the resultant Famine, then, devastated the country, although northern and eastern counties were not as badly affected (Johnson 1980:97; Silverman and Gulliver 1992; Dillon 1993:17). The Irish peasantry, in particular, had no other means of support, since their other crops (cabbage, carrots, and other root vegetables) were used by landlords in lieu of cash payment of rent. Without the potato crop, starvation was unavoidable. The English government, for the most part, refused effective aid to the Irish, believing that such aid would upset the free market. Such aid, the English further seemed to think, was not generally necessary: the Irish were starving, some said, because they were lazy (Johnson 1980:101–103). English politicians advocated a diminished governmental role so that natural market forces would be allowed to work, even in the face of massive starvation and crop failure.[10] It was not until four years into the Famine—1847—that the English government finally instituted soup kitchens. At the same time, grain, cattle, sheep, and other foodstuffs were being exported through Irish ports throughout the Famine, leading to considerable violence on the part of the Irish peasantry at times (Johnson 1980:103–104).

Even today informants tell stories of their ancestors' experiences in the Famine, dismissing soup kitchens run by either the government or Protestant churches as ineffective and cynical exercises. Both the few governmental relief programs and Protestant ministers fed the peasantry in their soup kitchens only if the Irish swore allegiance to Protestantism, giving up the Catholic Church; these converts became known as "soupers" or "soup Protestants." Informants say that Catholic priests forbade their parishioners to accept food or help of any kind from Protestants, though the Church had few resources to feed its faithful.

Exact mortality rates from the resultant starvation are difficult to find, but it is clear that the Famine drastically reduced the population of Ireland. Paul Johnson and other historians note that emigration, Famine-related diseases, cholera, and starvation reduced the Irish peasantry from over eight million in 1846 to under 4.5 million by 1901 (Johnson 1980:107–108). Emigration specifically was, and remains, a significant factor in the depopulation of Ireland, most emigrants (85%) going to the United States in the latter half of the nineteenth century (Johnson 1980:110; Dillon 1993:18).

In addition to the loss of nearly half the population of Ireland, the

Famine resulted in other deprivations for the Irish peasantry. Landlords apparently used the Famine to consolidate their estates, forcing small landholders to surrender their estates in return for food, or a place in the poorhouse (where many died), or passage out of the country (Johnson 1980:105). Some landlords offered no return at all, merely claiming their land back for planting or grazing, evicting their starving tenants. The Famine, and mass emigration, also effectively killed off the Irish language (Lee 1989; MacSiomóin 1994; Moane 1994); the language issue continues to occupy Irish intellectuals today.

It appears that the Catholic Church collaborated in the destruction of the Irish language. Prior to the Famine, the Church managed to obtain control of the schools; the 1831 National Education Scheme was run by priests, nuns, and brothers as part of the Church's interest in "civilizing" the Irish peasantry (Inglis 1987:121–125). In return for controlling the provision of a moral, Catholic education (at the time, almost exclusively to boys), the Church agreed to one requirement of the scheme: all classes were to be taught in English, with the use of "pagan," "savage" Irish forbidden (Johnson 1980:112–113). This is in accord with the Church's long resistance to Masses in the local vernacular, with the Latin Mass being abandoned only with Vatican II in the late 1960s. Interestingly, it was Protestant clergymen in the latter half of the nineteenth century who attempted to keep the Irish language alive, using it—mainly in the west of Ireland—as a language of conversion as well as a marker of Irish identity. When Catholic priests insisted on English, however, Irish was effectively dead (Johnson 1980: 113).

Retention of the native language was seen as less important by a growing Irish political movement than was liberation from English bonds. Landlords' and governmental actions during and after the Famine led to the formation of various groups demanding specific rights. The Irish Tenants Right League is one example of a political organization supported in part by covert and often violent actions against landlords (Dillon 1993:18). What is now the Irish Republican Army grew out of another political organization, the Irish Republican Brotherhood, or Fenians.[11] The Fenians mounted mainly ineffectual risings throughout the nineteenth century. The 1916 Easter rising was essentially a failure, since it garnered neither immediate relief from English rule nor widespread Irish support (Brown 1985; Johnson 1980).

MODERN IRELAND

It was not until December 1922, after increasingly crippling Irish attacks on English police and military positions, and after violent debates within Ireland, that the Treaty establishing the Irish Free State was signed (Johnson 1980:189–190; Brown 1985; Lee 1989). The six Ulster counties that now comprise Northern Ireland (the seventh county in the province, Donegal, is part of the Irish Republic) were not included in the Free State. A civil war in which the partition of Ulster was contested broke out almost immediately upon the signing of the Treaty but was more or less resolved by the election, in July 1923, of the political party favoring the Treaty (Johnson 1980:202; Brown 1985; Lee 1989), although, of course, Ulster continues the dispute internally to this day. The next fifteen years saw considerable political conflict within the Irish Free State, which remained part of the British Commonwealth until 1949.

The Irish Constitution was published in 1937, written, Irish Senator and historian Joseph Lee and most other Irish scholars argue, with the pervasive guidance of the Catholic Church (Lee 1989; Beale 1986). The Constitution, *Bunreacht na hÉireann*, which has been modified only slightly over the years, declares the Republic to be a Catholic country cherishing family life and motherhood (Article 41), political neutrality (Article 29),[12] and a parliamentary-style government based on proportional representation (Articles 15–27) (Constitution of Ireland 1990).

Evidence of Catholic influence can be seen throughout the Constitution. For example, Catholicism is evident in the Preamble to the Constitution. The writers of the Constitution appeal to one of the cornerstones of Catholic belief, the Holy Trinity of God the Father, God the Son, and God the Holy Spirit: "In the name of the Most Holy Trinity, from Whom is all authority and to Whom, as our final end, all actions of men and states must be referred, we the people of Éire, humbly acknowledging all our obligations to our Divine Lord, Jesus Christ, Who sustained our fathers through centuries of trial" (Preamble, Constitution of Ireland 1990). Catholic influence is also seen as the Constitution concludes with a prayerful invocation: *"Dochum Glóire Dé agus Onóra na hÉireann"* ("For the Glory of God and the Honor of Ireland") (Constitution of Ireland 1990:160). Further, the original Constitution, published in 1937, made note of the "special position" of the Catholic Church in Irish government in society as "the guardian of the faith of the great majority of the citizens" (Article 44, removed in 1972).[13] In addition, Irish sociologist Michelle Dillon notes that Church "influence extended from the immediate domain of marriage and sociosexual morality to inform also the formulation of education, health, and social policies, resulting in a church/state consensus on public morality that continued virtually undisturbed until the late 1970s" (Dillon 1993:24). The Catholic Church exerted considerable influence on politicians, almost all of whom were practicing Catholics, to pass legislation in accordance with Catholic doctrine.

The Mother and Child Scheme serves as an exemplar of direct

Church influence. The Minister of Health in the late 1940s, Noël Browne, proposed that the Irish government assume responsibility for the medical care of Irish mothers and children, something which the Catholic Church had been doing, as the Church ran all hospitals and medical clinics. Browne was bothered by the "primitive" level of care offered by Church-run medical facilities, noting that the falloff in vocations meant that there were fewer nuns and brothers available to perform medical work (Browne 1986:142). He suggested that there be mandatory testing and treatment for tuberculosis, mandatory medical examinations for all schoolchildren, an associated limitation on parental refusal to send children to school, and free health care and education to pregnant women and mothers (Browne 1986:150; Inglis 1987:60). The Church opposed any such measures, sending a letter to then-*Taioseach* (Prime Minister) Eamon de Valera that declared that "for the State, under the Act, to empower the public authority to provide for the health of all children, and to treat their ailments, and to educate women in regard to health, and to provide them with gynaecological services, was directly and entirely contrary to Catholic social teaching, the rights of the family, the rights of the Church in education, and the rights of the medical profession, and of voluntary institutions" (Browne 1986:152). Browne interprets this to mean that the Church was attempting to influence legislation after the bill was already under consideration. Browne remarks, in some amazement, that de Valera "made no attempt to protest about this clear intrusion by the bishops in a matter already decided on by the *Oireachtas* [the parliament]." (1986: 152). Browne then attempted to implement a modified Scheme.

He was summoned to the residence of Dublin Archbishop McQuaid[14] in October of 1950, after having been told by the Cabinet that "it was the practice, under Irish governmental protocol, for a minister to be expected to attend, when told to do so, at a bishop's palace" (Browne 1986:157). Browne attended the meeting, during which he was handed a letter from the bishops comprising the Irish Hierarchy; he reproduced the letter in its entirety in his autobiography. The bishops protested, in strong language, that the Mother and Child Scheme directly contradicted Catholic teaching. It read, in part:

> The right to provide for the physical education of children belongs in the family and not to the State. Experience has shown that physical or health education is closely interwoven with important moral questions on which the Catholic Church has definite teaching.
>
> Education in regard to motherhood includes instruction in regard to sex relations, chastity, and marriage. *The State has no competence to give instruction in such matters.*

. . . We have no guarantee that State officials will respect Catholic principles with regard to these matters. (Browne 1986:158, emphasis added)

The bishops argued that the State has only a limited role in family life; marriage, sex, education, and child rearing are Church matters. Surely this shows the Church intervening in what has been considered by social scientists to be "private."

Browne struggled on with his Scheme, defying the Church. His Cabinet colleagues, all elected to the Oireachtas, however, finally forced a resignation from Browne. His fellow ministers raged at him: one minister said, "How dare you invite me to disobey my church?"; another remarked that "As a Catholic, I obey my authorities"; a third insisted that "Those in the government who are Catholics are bound to accept the views of the Church" (Browne 1986:177). Browne was thrown out of office and publicly condemned by the bishops.

Although Hierarchy influence has waned considerably since the Mother and Child Scheme, in March 1995, Mr. Justice Rory O'Hanlon, a judge sitting on the Irish High Court, argued against a proposed *Dáil* (one of the houses of the Oireachtas, the parliament; see below) bill that would allow the dissemination of information regarding abortion facilities in Great Britain. Mr. Justice O'Hanlon's statement asserts that the Abortion Information Act should not be passed, since it is in contravention of the constitution: "Every piece of legislation enacted by the Oireachtas must be in conformity with the Constitution, that is to say, is enacted 'In the name of the Most Holy Trinity from Whom is all authority' and in the exercise of powers derived under God from the people" (O'Hanlon 1995:3). Since the Church opposes abortion, any information regarding abortion services would be not only morally wrong but unconstitutional, argued O'Hanlon. Although O'Hanlon was roundly criticized for his remarks on the very page where he presented them, the influence of the Catholic Church clearly continues to permeate Irish law and legislation if a judge on the Irish High Court feels free to comment on proposed legislation.

The postwar era found Ireland in economic malaise, dependent as it was on England, its primary trading partner at the time. There was an economic recovery in the 1960s and early 1970s (Crotty 1993:64–65), but the last 25 years have seen the Irish economy falter badly. The Irish governments of the past three decades have largely relied on multinational corporations to provide jobs in Ireland; there are few Irish corporations with sufficient productive capacity to ameliorate the current double-digit unemployment rate (*European Communities Encyclopedia and Directory* 1992:141), 17% when I was living there. Irish governmental social scientist Richard Breen and his colleagues at the Economic and Social Research Institute (ESRI), a government-funded but independent research group, report, however, that multinationals do not tend to remain in Ireland for more than ten years, and there is little to replace these employers (Breen et al. 1990:210–211).[15] An indigenous entrepreneurial spirit has been at best discouraged by postwar Irish governments. As will be discussed below, initiative tends to be squelched not only by governmental policy but by Irish cultural understandings regarding appropriate behaviors.

The history of Ireland, then, like so many others, is one of occupation. The Church, through St. Patrick, entered Ireland in the fifth century A.D. to convert the Irish to Catholicism. The Church invited the English in, partly for political reasons, and continues to attempt to directly control its flock through calls to faith and fidelity to Catholic belief, although overt political intervention has lessened to some extent. The English colonial presence, on the other hand, has waxed and waned throughout an eight-century occupation. It was not until the appearance of Oliver Cromwell on the scene that uniformly cruel and repressive actions emerged. The English oppression of the Irish reached its nadir with the Great Famine. The Great Hunger, more than anything else, marked the death knell of English colonialism in Ireland.

Today, the Irish continue to feel colonized, primarily through English and American electronic and print media. This, for the Irish, is a more insidious problem. Informants seemed unsure how to fight cultural colonialism, what many call the "coca-cola-ization" (and thus of American origin, as, of course, is Coca-Cola) of their country.

RECENT IRISH HISTORY AND CURRENT SOCIAL STRUCTURES

An examination of Irish political organization, as well as a detailed look at Irish perceptions of Church influence and clergy behavior, shows that informants continue to be affected by understandings about authority, accountability, and what is public and private. Political power is centralized, and there are few regional or local elected officials. There is little accountability in Irish politics, and little impetus to either request or provide more transparent governmental processes. Similarly, the decision-making processes of the Church were regarded by my informants as opaque; informants felt it was easier to ignore some Church dictates, particularly regarding sexual activity, than to openly challenge Church authority. This section discusses political and religious organization in the context of governmental and Church actions and authority patterns.

Politics

The Republic of Ireland has governmental, educational, economic, and social welfare systems similar to their former English overseers. That is, they are governed now by a bicameral parliament run by a prime minister, as the English are; the school systems run on similar schedules, with similar subjects and teaching techniques; and the Irish, like the English, have a generous social welfare system paid for in the main by a basic tax rate of 27% on earned income below IR£13,000 and 48% above that (Ardagh 1994:66). The Irish have welcomed, in addition, various technologies (e.g., television, radio, long-distance telephone services, faxes, e-mail and Internet interaction) now common in Western Europe and the United States. Those same technologies provide occasions for many Irish to grumble about cultural invasion by, primarily, the United States and its television programs. Fearing the tolerance if not adoption of poorly regarded American values, some informants commented freely on American values, which they interpret as glorifying violence, premarital and extramarital sex, divorce, disrespectful family relationships, selfish individualism, aggressively direct political confrontation, and capitalist consumerism. Irish society, declared informants, stands in opposition to American values.[16] That can be seen, partially, in an examination of Irish political organization.

Representative national government is provided by the Oireachtas, comprised of two houses, *Dáil Éireann* and *Seanad Éireann*. Members of both houses generally appear to place a premium on measured, rather than heated, debate; it seems that most decisions are made outside of house meetings (Ardagh 1994:45–48) (see below). The Dáil is an entirely elected body based on proportional representation (Constitution of Ireland, Article 16), while the Seanad is partly elected (49 members, including those elected by various university officials) and partly appointed (11 members) (Constitution of Ireland, Article 18). The appointed Seanad members are nominated by various governmental councils and civil servants, and, after consultation with the prime minister, the President makes the formal appointments to life terms. The Dáil has by far the most power in terms of legislation and national and European visibility; the Seanad by comparison acts more as an advisory body. The *Taoiseach*, or Prime Minister, is the leader of the political party that has won the most seats in the Dáil; he[17] must also be an elected member (*Teachta Dála*, or TD) of the Dáil. The deputy Prime Minister, or *Tánaiste*, must also be a TD. If the Taoiseach's party has a large enough majority, it is likely that the Tánaiste will be a member of that same party. However, in recent years, no political party has had a commanding majority, leading to a series of coalition governments.

There is an additional elected representative, *An tUachtarán*, the

President. The President holds a seven-year term and can be reelected once (Constitution of Ireland, Article 12.3). Presidential candidates are nominated by members of the Oireachtas or by members of the appointed County Councils, or a current eligible President may nominate himself (Constitution of Ireland, Article 12.4.2). The President has few official powers, his position equivalent in some ways to the German or Italian Presidency. He may speak to the nation if the TDs and Senators agree and approve the text of the message before it is delivered (Constitution of Ireland, Article 13.7); he may dissolve the parliament if the Taoiseach advises it (Constitution of Ireland, Article 13.2); but he must consult with and receive the approval of the parliament before performing any of these actions (Constitution of Ireland, Article 13.11). Although the President is ostensibly independently elected, he must watch what he says and what he does and "cannot say anything that might influence policy" (Ardagh 1994:59). This does provide some flexibility, however. The President during my stay in Ireland, Mary Robinson, used the Presidency to represent Ireland outside the country as an oblique way to make her views known; however, she was unwilling to discuss her personal views directly (which might influence policy) (Ardagh 1994:58).[18] The President has been only tangentially and subtly involved in current political issues, remaining above the fray of coalition politics.

In addition to fighting among partners in coalition governments—the Government of Albert Reynolds fell in November 1994 as a result of fierce disagreements between Fianna Fáil, the majority party, and Labour, a strong minority party and coalition partner—Irish politics is notorious for cronyism, personalism, corruption, and clientelism (Komito 1994; Ardagh 1994). Although, informants told me, the many civil service agencies in Ireland are, by and large, professional and honest, politicians are another story altogether. Anthropologist Lee Komito (1985, 1989, 1994) has written extensively about the personalized nature of Irish politics. He describes the day-to-day operation of Irish political machines, noting that TDs owe strong loyalties to their electorate. "Clients," or constituents, of a TD rely on him to bypass the bureaucratic process of the civil service, and clients ask the TD to expedite whatever the request might be. In Dublin, Komito says, this is particularly true among the working class (Komito 1994). TDs usually hold "clinics" in their area at least once a month and more usually once a week, so that the electorate, or, more accurately, the party faithful, can ask favors. The TDs tend, therefore, to look after their own constituency, with the result that, in effect, the Dáil acts less as a national body and more like a series of local interest groups (Ardagh 1994:45–48).

One effect of Irish clientism, as discussed above, is an interesting

blend of public activities—politics—with private concerns. A constituent may have a personal concern, one that would not affect anyone
outside her family. I was told of visits to a TD's clinic to ask the TD's
help in school admission, for example, or for waivers in zoning regulations for a house addition. The client regards the TD as an authority
figure, someone who can fix problems in return for the client's vote and
loyalty, and, very possibly, volunteer work around election time. If the
constituent does not support the TD or does not receive the service she
thinks she should, she withdraws but does not openly challenge the
TD. Personal concerns spark political contact for clients, a clear mixture of public and private arenas in the one case; in the other, like many
other Irish situations, people do not express dissatisfaction openly. Authority figures can take care of a person but cannot be challenged. This
set of understandings regarding political authority are also displayed
in Irish Catholic practice.

The TDs fill a need as they encourage clientism. The Republic has
no effective local government; all power, political, financial, and otherwise, is centered in Dublin. There is little town, county, or regional
government, and most of the crucial areas of people's everyday lives
are governed by appointed, not elected, officials who have accountability only to their sponsors. As Irish historian and member of the Seanad
Joseph Lee points out (1989), Ireland's is a centralized system, and the
center is Dublin. City and county councils can do little more than repair
roads, and even the funds for that must be begged from Dublin. There
are no elected school boards; instead, because of the Catholic majority
in and legislative control over the national schools, "boards of management," usually headed by a parish priest and composed of principals,
teachers, and a few compliant parents, are appointed by the diocesan
bishop. Ireland's entrance into the European Union in 1992 (Ireland
joined the EC in 1972) has meant another, even more distant layer of
authority exists: the EU in Brussels now hears requests for funding of,
for example, infrastructure projects and oversees disbursement and
completion. This insures that EU, not Irish, and certainly not local,
standards are met. Lack of local control is also seen in the fact that the
Irish police force, the *Garda Siochana* (also called "the Guards"), is
administered in Dublin, as well as in the organization of health services
into four regional boards, which are appointed by and accountable to
Dublin civil servants and not to residents of the regions. Cities and
towns, finally, elect mayors who have no legislative authority; city and
town managers are appointed.

In addition, surveys, as well as informants, confirm the centralization of authority as they hint at the effect of this. Data from the European Values Survey, the Irish part of which was conducted by social
scientists at the Economic and Social Research Institute (ESRI), dem-

onstrate that there is little interest in "public" political protest (Hardiman and Whelan 1994:113–114). The Survey separated political activities into two categories: conventional protest, which was defined as signing a petition or attending lawful demonstrations, and unconventional protest, defined as participating in unofficial strikes or occupying buildings or factories. Approximately 80% of the Irish respondents indicated that they had or would participate in conventional political activity, while the European average was about 70% (Hardiman and Whelan 1994:113). However, only 3% of Irish respondents said that they had participated in more direct political protest, compared to 6% of the other Europeans surveyed—twice as many (Hardiman and Whelan 1994). Researchers from ESRI, who are Irish themselves, interpret this to reflect their respondents' belief "that they have no political influence" (Hardiman and Whelan 1994:116). We should note that the Irish responses were not unusual in European terms, something which the ESRI researchers attribute to the inadequacy of the Survey instrument for the nature of Irish politics: "Activities such as contacting constituency TDs, in person or in writing, or lodging a protest with the relevant minister or department, are not considered. Extensive use is made of contact with local politicians for a whole variety of objectives, arguably to a greater degree than in most democratic politics . . ." (Hardiman and Whelan 1994:112). Irish scholars, then, note that the Irish perceive themselves as powerless, partly because politics are centralized.

The centralization of political power in Dublin, reminiscent of English colonial political structures in Ireland, parallels the Catholic Church's organization. Although the seat of power for the Church is actually in Armagh (in Northern Ireland), there is an interesting correspondence between political and religious establishments in Ireland. The Church in Ireland is a hierarchical system, ultimately answerable to the Papal Nuncio—the Vatican's appointed representative—resident in Ireland. Of course, the religious community is not elected by the Catholics it serves and so reports to Church authorities, the bishops, known as the Hierarchy. This means that priests, nuns, religious brothers, and monks are accountable to bishops, archbishops, and cardinals, who are accountable in turn to the Vatican, through the Nuncio. No one is accountable to the Catholic laity—and the laity does not demand transparency. Appointed authorities, rather than elected ones, hold most of the overall power in Ireland, whether that power is educational, political, economic, or religious.

This lack of accountability of the Church and most government officials to the Irish populace was demonstrated through several events during the course of my fieldwork (September 1993–March 1995). The fall of Albert Reynolds's coalition government in November 1994 in part

hinged on the insistence of Dick Spring, the leader of the Labour party
(partner with Fianna Fáil, Reynolds's party, in government), for more
"transparent" and "accountable" government. I watched the events un-
fold in both the print and electronic media over the course of several
weeks, and informants discussed it often. The story seemed to involve
a change in understandings about political behavior. Reynolds decided
to appoint Harry Whelehan to the Presidency of the Supreme Court.
Whelehan was at that time Ireland's Attorney General. He had been
responsible for a Constitutional crisis after what was seen as his heavy-
handed treatment of a statutory rape/abortion case (the "Miss X" case;
see O'Reilly 1992 for a complete discussion). Reynolds appointed Whelehan to the Presidency of the Supreme Court over Labour's objec-
tions.[19] Spring took advantage of the situation and in effect dissolved
the government by declaring in the Dáil that, should it come down to
it (not that he was suggesting it), he would cast a "no confidence" vote.
Arguing that an elected representative—the Taoiseach—in a coalition
government should not and cannot make unilateral decisions, Spring
called for a new day in Irish politics, in which representatives would
truly represent and not just rule. Spring's declaration that there was
a need for a different kind of Irish politics, one in which accountability
dominates, in which politics is an open (public?) process and in which
authority can and should be challenged, provoked defensive responses
by Reynolds and his party members (who were ultimately defeated).
The fact that Reynolds objected to Spring's characterization of Irish
politics demonstrates, at least partly, that Irish political culture has
revolved around unquestioned authority and a special understanding
of political activity as conducted secretly until very recently.

The Catholic Church Hierarchy

Unlike the authority of Irish politicians, the authority structure in
the Catholic Church in Ireland remains strong. Sex scandals and ref-
erenda on social issues which the Church considers its province show
that the Hierarchy continues to influence political and personal understandings even as the Church has retreated from direct legislative intervention. The Mother and Child Scheme debate in the late 1940s was
perhaps the quintessential example, after the publication of the original constitution, of overt Church influence.

The Church has changed its method of influencing legislation to some
extent. Irish sociologist Michelle Dillon explores the 1986 divorce referendum, which was rejected by Irish voters 64% to 36% (Dillon 1993:
2).[20] Divorce is expressly forbidden by the Church (Catechism of the
Catholic Church 1994:§1650–1651 and §2382). Dillon examines the influence of the Irish Hierarchy, as well as that of the media, Irish fem-

inists, and political debate, in the defeat of the 1986 referendum. Dillon concludes that the Church did not cause the failure of the referendum, but it certainly influenced the outcome. Although the Hierarchy, by the 1980s, had altered its role from legislative framer to social critic and advisor, the bishops still had a good deal to say to their flock about divorce. The bishops asserted that they supported a separation between church morality and state business, but parish priests had a duty to argue against the divorce referendum at the pulpit and to offer the Church's moral teachings and Christ's position on marriage and divorce (Dillon 1993:95). At the same time, the bishops' official line was that the individual Catholic was free to make a choice regarding the vote after consulting his own conscience (Dillon 1993:94).

There were dissident voices in the Hierarchy, though, who opposed the post–Vatican II emphasis on individual conscience and a personal set of ethics that resulted in the Hierarchy's noninterventionist stance. Bishops McNamara (Dublin), O'Sullivan (Kerry) and Newman (Limerick) all provided statements to the media and to Irish Catholics at Mass that divorce fundamentally violated basic Catholic moral and social precepts (Dillon 1993:97–98). And a theologian from Kimmage Manor, a missionary seminary on the south side of Dublin, declared that no Catholic, legislator or simple citizen, could vote for a referendum that was contrary to Catholic teachings (Dillon 1993:100). It should be noted, however, that other theologians argued that voters should consider the referendum in light of social need, individual rights, and the common good, all of which are historically variable and thus not subject to Hierarchy moral judgment (Dillon 1993:99).

Dillon analyzes the dissension in the ranks of the Hierarchy, and in academic theology, as a marker of the Church's changed position in Irish politics and society. While during much of the century the Hierarchy encouraged, if not pressured, legislators to enact laws in conformance with Catholic teachings, by the 1980s the Hierarchy, officially at any rate, had significantly repositioned itself in Irish society. Most of the bishops attempted to take seriously post–Vatican II values such as the development of individual ethical systems and separation of church and state. However, not all of the Hierarchy agreed, encouraged perhaps by the conservatism of John Paul II (Dillon 1993:102; Hornsby-Smith and Whelan 1994:16–18; Inglis 1987:15). What Dillon finds remarkable is that this dissension was aired in the media (Dillon 1993: 104). She sees this as related to a growing Church tendency to discuss moral and social concerns within a secular framework of sociological and demographic evidence: "the more the Church endorses the separation of church and state, the more it uses secular discourse in presenting its teaching" (Dillon 1993:105). Dillon believes, however, that Irish voters did not believe the Church's use of secular evidence: "people appeared to treat its nonreligious pronouncements as though they were still doctrinally grounded" (Dillon 1993:109). This meant that Irish Catholics lost the opportunity to engage in challenges to, or at least discussions with, the Church's position. Dillon concludes that Irish voters perceived the Catholic Church in the 1986 divorce referendum to be making authoritative, immutable statements that could not be questioned. Even though the Church had, on the face of it, altered its approach to political issues, Irish Catholics responded without engaging their Church in sincere discussion. This unwillingness to participate in open challenges to established Church authority is also seen in recent well-publicized cases of priestly sex behavior, repeatedly discussed by informants as well as Irish media while I was in the field.

The widely discussed Bishop Casey affair had the potential to challenge Church authority in Ireland, but the Hierarchy ultimately protected its own. In 1992, allegations regarding the behavior of Dr. Éamonn Casey, Bishop of Galway, arose: he apparently had an eighteen-month sexual relationship with Annie Murphy, a young Irish-American, in the early 1970s. She became pregnant and kept the boy she bore. Bishop Casey paid child support out of diocesan funds but refused contact with the child (McGarry 1997; Ardagh 1994:167–171). After hiding this affair for nearly twenty years, his girlfriend finally revealed it. Casey admitted to the affair a few days after the public revelation and immediately resigned; he is now a missionary priest in Ecuador, although he returns to Ireland frequently. My informants thought that the Casey affair raised issues of priestly celibacy and hypocrisy—since Casey had long preached on the evils of extramarital sex while engaging in such activities himself—but, at the same time, parishioners in Casey's diocese raised more than IR£100,000 to repay the IR£70,000 Casey appropriated from diocesan funds to keep Murphy silent.

During a visit to Ireland in 1992, I discovered a great ambivalence among Irish Catholics concerning the Bishop Casey affair. On the one hand, many with whom I spoke seemed to think that Casey's behavior was not very surprising, since, they said, priests do what they want regardless of what they preach. There was a double standard, according to the Irish people I talked to. On the other hand, however, one person said, "well, he's only human, isn't he. Sure what's the problem anyway?" The latter comment goes a long way in explaining Casey's successful fund-raising activities: when it comes to the Church, the Irish forgive a good deal. One priest told me that, although the Casey affair provoked some questions within the Church regarding celibacy, those discussions were rarely shared with people outside the religious community; that, too, was forgiven.

Members of the Hierarchy continue to behave with little regard for the everyday Catholic's opinion, and the everyday Catholic does not challenge the Hierarchy. While I was in the field, several sex scandals came to light. One, the Brendan Smyth affair, I discuss below. Another involved the fatal heart attack of a parish priest (serving in suburban Dublin) at a notorious gay sauna in the city centre of Dublin, despite the Church's official positions requiring priestly celibacy and forbidding homosexual activity for anyone (*Minneapolis Star-Tribune* 1994:13A). Though my informants all rather gleefully discussed this incident, briefly giggling at what they saw as Church hypocrisy, that hypocrisy did not seem to challenge fundamentally their identification with the Church. "There's no point to arguing wit' 'em," one Dubliner told me, "them priests'll do what they will." Nonetheless, this informant continued to go to Mass, keeping his thoughts about the Church to himself, or, at least, far from the Hierarchy.

The Church seems to have successfully defended itself, although only after some prodding, against another sex scandal. Father Brendan Smyth, who died in August 1997 while serving time in jail for child sexual abuse, apparently engaged in extensive sexual abuse with young parishioners, male and female, over a period of forty years. The Irish media discovered that the Irish Catholic Church was aware of Father Smyth's activities; whenever allegations were made, the media reported, his Abbot moved him to a different parish. Garda (police) contact was not made by Church officials in the Republic; he was finally arrested, tried, and convicted in Northern Ireland when Belfast Catholic parents, upon learning of their children's abuse, decided to ignore the Church and go to the police. Father Smyth and the American Catholic Church have been successfully sued by Smyth's victims in the United States in addition to his criminal prosecution in Northern Ireland (Haughey 1997b). Only recently have Irish victims contemplated civil suits totaling IR£1.5 million (Haughey 1997a). The Hierarchy denied that it had or should have had any knowledge of Smyth's activities, since he reported not to Armagh but to an independent monastery. Finally, however, in late 1994, more than a year after the scandal broke, the then-Archbishop of Armagh and Primate of All Ireland, Cardinal Cahal Daly, apologized to Smyth's victims and to Irish Catholics in general, admitting responsibility despite his contention that he had no direct knowledge of the incidents. Most of my informants seemed happy enough with the apology, seeing Smyth's behavior as a result of his individual mental illness and certainly not a systemic problem. A few informants, however, were moved by this set of events to discuss "funny" priests or religious brothers who tried to molest and beat them when the informants were young boys or girls. None of these informants ever told anyone about the molestation: "Ah no, if I had told me mam, she'd've swot me for tellin' tales and thinking dirty; I deserved it probably anyway," one man in his midthirties told me. The Irish Catholic Church, then, like the Irish political system, remains unaccountable to its constituents. Irish people rarely directly challenge either their priests or their politicians, and they make few overt demands for change.

Although some Catholics have only very recently begun to challenge Church officials (Pollak 1996a), Church teachings discourage questioning by Catholic lay people (Hornsby-Smith and Whelan 1994:16; Dillon 1993:98). So, for example, parishioners are not encouraged to read the Bible for themselves. In everyday practice, the priest interprets the texts, by way of his weekly homily (sermon) for Catholics.[21] The priest represents Christ: the Catechism of the Catholic Church declares that the priesthood "has the task not only of representing Christ—Head of the Church—before the assembly of the faithful, but also acting in the name of the whole Church when presenting to God the prayer of the Church, and above all when offering the Eucharistic sacrifice" (*Catechism of the Catholic Church* 1994:§1552). It is the priest, like Christ, who will tell you how to behave, what to think, and how to believe: the Catechism states that priests are "consecrated in order to preach the Gospel and shepherd the faithful" (*Catechism of the Catholic Church*: §1564). As we have seen in the discussion of the Mother and Child Scheme and, to a lesser extent, the 1986 divorce referendum, Catholic doctrine teaches that one should not question a priest or other religious, just as one does not question Christ: the Catechism of the Catholic Church declares that "the faithful receive with docility the teachings and directives that their pastors give them in different forms" (*Catechism of the Catholic Church* 1994:§87). In Catholicism, direct interaction between a believer and God, unlike in most Protestant credos, should be mediated by a priest or a saint, exemplified by the sacrament of Confession, in which a penitent admits sins to the priest, who then metes out penance in his position as Christ's representative. Regular performance of the Transubstantiation, the purpose of Mass, in which bread and wine are transformed into Christ's body and blood, is a basic requirement of the priesthood (*Catechism of the Catholic Church* 1994: §1552). Therefore, much of the Church concerns obeying authority and accepting God's will as interpreted by the Hierarchy and the priesthood.

Not all Catholics follow the Church's lead, of course. One informant, a firm believer, had strong views on the Church:

> The Church isn't the priests and the nuns and the brothers. It's the people, and the people are beautiful. They're the diamonds in the rough. Jesus said it, that the Church is the people. The priests, the nuns, they don't really matter; they feck the whole

thing up a lot of the time. It's the people who matter, it's them that make the Church beautiful. I firmly believe that. Like a few years ago, I got the snip [a vasectomy] 'cause we didn't want any more children, and an auld wan, a priest I know, told me I couldn't receive the Sacraments any more. What a load of shite! I'm still the same man, I still feel the spirit, and I don't care what the priest says. The Church is important to me, very important to me, but despite the clergy.[22]

This man, however, did not confront the priest and tell him that the Church's interpretation of "the snip" was wrong. My informant simply continued going to Mass and continued to receive the Sacraments. His wife, on the other hand, does not attend Mass very much any more, although she refused to discuss her reasons.

Another informant has stopped going to church completely. She finds nothing good about the Church at all:

The Catholic Church thrives on fear. Fear of exclusion. Confirmation[23] is all about that. If you don't get confirmed, you'll be excluded. All your schoolmates are going to special classes, and if the bishop asks you a question about the Catechism and you get it wrong, you can be refused Confirmation. You're bullied into learning Catechism by memory because if you don't you won't be allowed in. The Church is bullying, and it's violent. The bishop, when you're confirmed, gives you a slap. Yeah, it's a tap but it's symbolic. Hitting is acceptable, and you're grateful for it when a superior does it. If someone in charge bullies you it's okay. That's what the Church does—it's do as I say not as I do . . . Confession is just more of fear. Confession is about telling your mistakes to someone who will punish you, and you have to atone for your sins even if the priest is a total eejit [idiot]. The Church just wants you afraid because then you won't ask questions. And if you ask questions, if you challenge them, they get upset and say it's against the natural order of things.

This woman is unusual in her analysis of what she sees as Church cruelty and violence; most other Irish people I knew did not discuss the Church in any kind of detail, uninterested in criticism. This informant, however, has lived in Great Britain and additionally has been in psychotherapy, which may account in part for her analysis. She clearly holds a negative view of the Church.

Despite a massive falloff in church attendance, Catholicism remains emotionally and spiritually important for large numbers of Irish people. The European Values Survey, mentioned above, shows that 97% of

Irish people surveyed identified themselves as Roman Catholics
(Hornsby-Smith and Whelan 1994:20–21). Moreover, 80% of all respondents reported at the time that they attend Mass at least once a week
(Hornsby-Smith and Whelan 1994:23); almost all of my informants did
as well. Although priest friends in the cities of Dublin and Limerick
said that their Masses are rarely filled to even 10% capacity, rural practice seems to be higher (Taylor 1995:21–22). Still, the Church in Ireland, as in so many other countries, is in trouble. Despite the fact that
priests, nuns, and the Hierarchy in general are rarely, if ever, directly
challenged—in fact, the news media in general has treated the Hierarchy with kid gloves until very recently—a good deal of quiet grum-
bling goes on.

This is reflected in recent surveys examining Irish attitudes toward
religion, reported in the *Irish Times* on line (Pollak 1996b; O'Sullivan
1998). For instance, weekly Mass attendance has dropped, on average,
to 60% of respondents; fifteen years ago, it was 87% (O'Sullivan 1998).
Furthermore, Irish Catholics seem to be secularizing: the survey indicates that less than a quarter of those questioned follow Church dictates, electing to trust their own moral conscience (Pollak 1996b).
Finally, a 1998 survey shows that 40% of Irish Catholics questioned
"rarely or never go to confession" (O'Sullivan 1998). This is an aston-
ishing change even in the three years since I left Ireland. Indeed, the
Irish Times web site (http://www.irish-times.com/), on line only since
1996, seems to have a story critical of the Church in almost every edition. I left Ireland in 1995, when few people publicly confronted the
Church. It appears that a small minority are now beginning to challenge the Hierarchy. Surveys seem to show that this is in part due to
the many sexual abuse and sexual activity scandals involving priests;
respondents said that these scandals damaged the Church significantly
(O'Sullivan 1998). Overall, however, my impression is that the Irish,
in the main, are simply leaving the Church to itself rather than con-
fronting Catholicism directly.

The Irish do not make direct or overt challenges, feeling powerless
to change or stop the Church's actions, indicating that the Irish understanding of what "public" is differs considerably from other Western
societies, as well as from many non-Western societies. That is, many
Irish people consider their dissatisfactions or disagreements with the
Church—or, for that matter, with Irish politicians—to be private, personal, and purposeless. There is a fatalism, linked to a lack of trust in
authorities both secular and religious as well as understandings involving equality and envy, which keeps many Irish people from acting
in openly conflictual ways. We turn now to look at some basic Irish
cultural understandings that pervade much of social life as I describe
the few ethnographies of Ireland that have been done.

NOTES

1. One interesting aspect of Irish scholarship concerns the complex inter-relationship of academic, governmental, clerical, and journalistic networks, most of which are centered in Dublin and, to a lesser extent, Cork. One college professor (head of his department) I knew also served on appointed official governmental "cultural" boards; he had a large budget and determined governmental policy and expenditures for artistic endeavors. Several professors also serve as representatives in the parliament; Joseph Lee and David Norris are the most prominent. The *Irish Independent* publishes regular Sunday columns by other representatives such as Michael McDowell, while the *Irish Times* publishes articles by parliamentary representatives on an irregular basis. Elizabeth Sheehan, an ethnographer of the Irish intelligentsia, describes this network: "It is of more than passing interest to an ethnographer to know that a number of a country's now middle-aged academics, writers, judges, and politicians were members of the same university cohort and have all been involved with the same woman" (Sheehan 1993:79). It is an oversimplification to say that Irish government is Irish journalism is Irish academia; but the extraordinarily close-knit community of powerful men arguably has a strong influence on important areas of Irish culture, particularly because this community is informally but publicly acknowledged as existing. It is not a secret.

2. There are, of course, other influences that have shaped and continue to shape Irish cultural understandings. Because of the Church's long history in Ireland, discussed below, and because the Irish still identify themselves in the ideal if not the reality as devoutly Catholic, I discuss the Church in some detail here.

3. So, for example, the Catholic Church forbids "artificial" contraception such as the various birth control pills, the diaphragm, the IUD, the condom, or the "morning-after" pill, saying that any method that as a consequence will " 'render procreation impossible' is intrinsically evil" (*Catechism of the Catholic Church* 1994:§2370). A Dublin gynecologist and an Irish psychiatrist separately told me, however, that although use of the Pill for contraceptive use was illegal until the late 1970s, it could be prescribed for menstrual difficulties such as heavy bleeding, excessive pain, or other difficult physical symptoms. The gynecologist laughingly remarked that Irish women, in her experience, had the highest rate of dysmennorrhea in the world. Despite this, Irish Catholics seem to have followed Church dictates with regard to family size until recently; Scheper-Hughes notes that, in rural Ireland, the average family size in 1924 was 6.1 children and in 1974 was 4.1 (Scheper-Hughes 1979:138). Similarly, Humphreys, an ethnographer of Dublin in the late 1940s, says that urban families had, on average, between 3.5 and 4.0 children per family (Humphreys 1966:78–79). The current Irish fertility rate has dropped from 3.5 children per family in 1977 to 2.1 children in 1993 (World Bank 1995:366–367). Although I can only speculate from the reduction in family size, since informants were extremely uncomfortable discussing sex and contraception, it appears that despite Church dictates, men and women are finding ways to limit family size. One young adult informant in her early twenties and unmarried, whose fifty-

year-old mother was one of 22 surviving children (my informant's grandmother, apparently, had delivered more than 30 times), told me with some vigor that she would have, at most, two children. However, this young woman repeatedly declared this to me in what seemed to be defensive tones, indicating that she was not entirely comfortable with defying Church doctrine with regard to birth control and family size.

4. It is important to refrain from overstating the case. I am arguing that the Catholic Church and Irish political history and current political structure are connected with current Irish cultural understandings concerning what is private and what is public. I am *not* arguing that the Church and politics have *determined* Irish culture.

5. Most historical studies written by Irish scholars present this view as well. See, for instance, Johnson 1980; Brown 1985; Inglis 1987; Lee 1989; and Dillon 1993.

6. Viking raids were a constant danger from 800 to 1200; Dublin and Limerick, in particular, were founded or expanded by the rapacious Vikings. It is puzzling that Vikings are not interpreted by Irish historians as colonizers, although it appears that the Vikings initially acted more violently as colonizers than did the English.

7. Moane (1994) notes that English occupation of Ireland began much earlier than its other colonial activities and that it ended relatively earlier in comparison to other colonies (Moane 1994:253–256).

8. Any mention of Cromwell drew an immediate sneer to the faces of informants. One woman, who was originally from one of the counties bordering Northern Ireland, discussed Cromwell with a vituperous vehemance, as if he still oppressed the Catholic peasantry. History elicits highly emotional reactions, and some of my informants continue to express violent sentiments toward the English even as they deplore sectarian violence in the North. As the father of my own American ancestor was hanged in England in 1649 for consorting with a Cromwell—Thomas, not Oliver—this was discomfiting, to say the least. Some informants viewed me with a little suspicion after I revealed the relationship, and it took some time and quite a bit of explanation to repair friendships.

9. Loyalty oaths such as Johnson describes here show an interesting demarcation of definitions of public and private. Catholic behavior became semisecret, known to fellow Catholics but not to "public" authorities. This may have affected how the Church began to understand its responsibilities toward parishioners. If Catholics swore secret oaths only in the presence of trusted other Catholics, political as well as religious activity and statuses could have become understood as more public in the presence of a specifically designated community but not to the government. Political and religious activity then might have taken on a special watchfulness for Catholics, in which other Catholics and not the state were responsible for judging behavior. There could be a connection between this and the Church's emerging understandings about what is appropriately private and public. Irish history has not, of course, *determined* current Irish culture, but neither should its importance be underestimated.

10. Dillon (1993) asserts that the English government handled the Famine based on its own concerns with profitable industrialization: "Most of Ireland

was reserved primarily to function as Britain's farmyard, as a supplier of food for Britain's industrial classes, thus suppressing its own internal industrial development. The profits from Irish agricultural production were used by the British government to finance its own industrial growth as well as that of the Protestant, northern region of Ireland where, from the eighteenth century, industrialization was also pursued" (Dillon 1993:16). English colonial policy dictated that most of Ireland remain agrarian so that the English working class would be fed, even during the Famine.

11. "Fenian" remains an epithet still hurled at Catholics and citizens of the Republic. During my fieldwork, in January 1995, I watched, with some informants, a televised Dublin football "friendly," a soccer match between the Republic of Ireland and English World Cup teams, which ended within the first few minutes of play as English fans (some of whom, it turned out, were neo-Nazis) began rioting, shouting "Fenian bastards," among other things, at the Irish fans. Matches between the Republic of Ireland and Northern Ireland teams have had similar results. The term "Fenian" has undeniable emotional power a century after its coining. My informants were offended by the English use of "Fenian" as we watched this match together; they told me it was not insulting if used by Irish Catholics. We can compare this to the African-American appropriation of "nigger" or the gay community's use of "queer."

12. So, for example, Belfast was bombed heavily during World War II, one elderly informant told me, but Dublin was largely left alone by the Germans. However, my informant also pointed out that it was Dublin fire-fighting crews who raced to the scene to help.

13. Irish social scientists assert that the Church's political influence has waned dramatically in the past twenty years (Hornsby-Smith and Whelan 1994:18–19). For example, in 1979, prohibitions on the sale of contraceptives were lifted, in direct contravention of Catholic doctrine then and now; in 1992, a ban on traveling outside Ireland to get an abortion was lifted, against Catholic doctrine; and in December 1995, the ban on divorce was repealed. The Church opposed all measures.

14. Bishop McQuaid is notorious for forbidding Catholics to attend Trinity College Dublin, associated with Protestantism (Trinity did not admit Catholic students until after the establishment of the Irish Free State). Bishop McQuaid forbade Catholic attendance at this ostensibly Protestant university "under pain of mortal sin" (Browne 1986:142)—that is, sin that can never be forgiven.

15. Breen, Hornsby, Whelan, Hardiman, Cassells, and Crotty, all cited herein, are social scientists attached to the Economic and Social Research Institute (ESRI). This group describes itself as "an independent, non–profit-making body" which "conducts research by its own staff in close cooperation with the universities and other organisations" (Institute of Public Administration Yearbook 1994:346); most books and pamphlets analyzing Irish society that are available are sponsored by ESRI. The social scientists have immediate access to data and libraries unavailable to most other researchers. I rely on their generally balanced presentation of census and other governmental data when that data was difficult for me to obtain.

16. One informant described the trouble American society is in, listing a plethora of social ills and commenting on the lack of real "character" on the

part of the American people. I remarked that he must know many Americans given his knowledge of American society. "Well, no," he replied, "I watch *Oprah*." Most Irish people, like most other non-American people, seem to get their information about American society through television.

17. Although there is no prohibition in the Constitution with regard to a woman becoming Taoiseach, to date no woman has been elected by fellow TDs to the position.

18. I found only one person who spoke against Mary Robinson, who suspected that Robinson did not care about Ireland but about becoming U.N. Secretary General (indeed, the rumor then was that her name was on the short list; she has been appointed the U.N. representative for Human Rights). Otherwise, "our Mary" was universally and enthusiastically supported by all informants. Even if they disagreed with Robinson's support of birth control availability and other feminist concerns, voters in November 1990 apparently saw her as "representing a new, more modern and liberal Ireland" (Ardagh 1994:56).

19. Whelehan was eventually "persuaded" to forgo his new post, though his decision was not reached until several weeks after his official appointment. Video and still prints of his appointment, which the president, Mary Robinson, was forced to rubber-stamp, show President Robinson's clear disapproval of the situation through stiff body language and hollow smiles. The press made much of Robinson's demeanor.

20. Another constitutional referendum on divorce was held on November 24, 1995; it passed by a margin of less than one half of a percentage point (Anderson 1995: section 2, p. 1). I discuss political and constitutional understandings of marriage and divorce below.

21. I base the observations regarding Catholic practice in this section in part on my own Catholic upbringing and my experience in Irish Catholic Churches.

22. "Feck" and "shite" are polite forms of "fuck" and "shit."

23. Confirmation is a Sacrament conferred after Catholics have been baptized (2–3 months after birth) and have performed their first Confession and Communion (at age 7 or so). It marks adult membership in the Church and should be conferred at "the age of reason" (Catechism of the Catholic Church 1994:§1307) and typically takes place at around age 12. After learning an advanced catechism, confirmands are anointed with oil and slapped on the cheek by the bishop.

CHAPTER 3

Don't Be Greedy

As we have seen, Irish history and social institutions—politics and religion—combine to influence relationships in which Irish people make few overt demands or challenges. An examination of Irish ethnography and anthropological analysis demonstrates how some of these cultural understandings play out in day-to-day life. The Irish set of behaviors, called "begrudgery," illustrates this particularly well. Here I look at the treatment of Ireland in ethnographic literature and discuss some salient cultural understandings.

THE ANTHROPOLOGICAL PICTURE OF IRELAND

The well-known ethnographers (primarily American, and a few British, scholars) of Ireland have paid scant attention to the subject of authority structures in both urban and rural areas, focusing instead on the rural Irish. From Conrad Arensberg (1937) and his partner Solon Kimball (Arensberg and Kimball 1968) through Hugh Brody (1973), Nancy Scheper-Hughes (1979), and John Messenger (1983, 1989), the cultural, psychological, and social effects of English occupation and Church attendance and belief are not addressed, with the exception of the sensitive ethnographic treatments of Irish Catholicism by American Larry Taylor (Taylor 1980, 1989a, 1989b, and 1995).[1] Instead, the curious habits of Irish peasants gain center stage. Certainly urban life is rarely addressed; the only full-length ethnography regarding cities in the Republic is Alexander Humphreys', based on sociological field-work done in the late 1940s among working-class Dubliners (Humphreys 1966).[2]

Almost all earlier ethnographers of the Republic of Ireland have chosen field sites deep in rural Ireland, in small agrarian Irish-speaking communities (the *Gaeltacht*) (Arensberg 1937; Arensberg and Kimball 1968; Brody 1973; Shanklin 1975; Fox 1978; Kane 1977, 1979; Scheper-Hughes 1979; Messenger 1983, 1989; Curtin, Kelly, and O'Dowd 1984; Curtin, Jackson, and O'Connor 1987; Taylor 1995). These studies have tended, until very recently, to paint rural Ireland as consisting of either stable face-to-face peasant societies (Arensberg 1937; Arensberg and Kimball 1968) or depressed, declining face-to-face peasant societies (Brody 1973; Fox 1978; Scheper-Hughes 1979; Messenger 1983). Focusing on emigration, dispirited and schizophrenogenic relationships, economic difficulties, and the cloying and socially and emotionally inhibiting nature of rural village life, these ethnographers located their work in areas that were and are considered to be unusual by many Irish people outside these isolated areas (Kane, personal communication; Walsh, personal communication). Dermot Walsh, the psychiatrist in charge of all Irish mental health services, in addition, points out that Scheper-Hughes' study detailing the "death of Ireland" (Scheper-Hughes 1979:xv), linking schizophrenia to rural economic decline, took place in a time "when Ireland had never been more prosperous" (Walsh 1991:35.). Even Taylor (1995) acknowledges, in his otherwise splendid ethnography of Irish Catholics, that he chose his field site in rural Donegal, seeking a *Gaeltacht* (where Irish is spoken as a first language) that would contain "a 'traditional' local culture different enough to attract the attention of the anthropologist and perhaps able to shed light on earlier European cultural forms" (Taylor 1995:22). Like his earlier ethnographer colleagues, Taylor chose Donegal for its differentness. The ethnographers of rural Ireland further tend to represent their studies as representative of all of Irish culture, in that all of them refer to the "Irish" and "Irish culture" as if the West of Ireland was typical. The result of anthropological emphasis on rural cultural understandings, despite the fact that nearly two-thirds of Irish people live in towns or cities,[3] is an incomplete picture of the Republic as a whole.[4]

Most ethnographers of Ireland tend to describe "the Irish" as rather simple yet devious folk living in either tightly knit or depopulated communities. Messenger's study of the Aran Islands, off the coast of Galway (Messenger 1983), for instance, portrays Aran Islanders as superstitious, slavishly Catholic, drunken innocents who tell a great story. The people Messenger describes apparently are remnants of a prehistoric Celtic past. Scheper-Hughes, on the other hand, attempts to show the psychopathological effects of what she saw as desperate poverty in rural Kerry but which she calls "Irish culture" (Scheper-Hughes 1979).

BEGRUDGERY AND SLAGGING

What is clear, however, from the various ethnographies of Ireland is that there are certain general behavioral patterns among the Irish, many of which are connected with the extraordinary sociability of many Irish people. Even in Dublin, a city of 1.5 million people, many people belong to long-standing kin and friendship networks. Most of social life takes place within those networks, although newcomers are not shunned as long as they have the proper sponsorship. This means that much of Irish social life in Dublin takes place in a series of face-to-face communities. There is more opportunity in Dublin, however, to escape those networks and to form or join new ones through church, school, work, university attendance, or social clubs,[5] than there is in small villages.

In such face-to-face networks, tensions invariably arise. Several different behavioral patterns help people cope with disagreement and what is experienced, though not articulated, as limited resources (economic, social, sexual, and psychological). Many of my informants, for example, as well as various columnists in Sunday papers, regularly discussed "begrudgery" rather freely as an Irish trait (a discussion regarding begrudgery and intimacy appears in Chapter 8). Begrudgery is more than simple envy at another's good fortune. It is an intent to flatten social differences, aimed at insuring everyone's equality within a community. If someone gains something, another person is sure to lose somehow. Irish historian and senator Joe Lee puts it this way: "For many, keeping the other fellow down offered the surest defense of their own position" (Lee 1989:646).

One informant told me of his struggles to start an innovative business in his large town (5,000+ in the eastern part of Ireland). Parents, siblings, friends, and community leaders have all discouraged his attempts, telling him how it was going to fail. This man railed against his community's unwillingness to try new things, at the fear of failing, at warnings that he was "getting too big for his boots" and that he very likely would be sorely disappointed. My informant called begrudgery "the psychology of the lowest common denominator." At the same time, he said, begrudgery is the way that everyone remains the same: no one is too much better (and if someone tries, he is heavily discouraged) but, at the same time, no one is too much worse.

My informant was told more or less directly to stop trying to better himself, but there are other ways to level as well, again verified by ethnography. "Slagging" is one method the Irish use to guarantee equality in social life.[6] An Irish person will joke with a companion about the companion's foibles, using specific examples, which will be known in the community, given the frequent interaction most Irish people have with each other. These jokes, while quite funny, are double-edged and can be interpreted as insulting. In essence, slagging is an elaborate form of teasing.[7]

The proper response to slagging is to laugh at oneself while "getting back" at one's slagger. Most people whom I observed knew how far to go, and they stopped short of being truly hurtful. This in turn allowed the recipient to show proper Irish behavior by not displaying hurt feelings. In Dublin, if one is truly insulted or hurt, a quiet statement to that effect ends the round of slagging. Most of the time, though, slagging serves not only the more confining purposes of leveling but also can be a plain marker of intimacy, friendship, and acceptance.[8] A person must know another quite well to be able to choose an effective slag. That sort of relationship means that the slagger will not go too far, and she will stop if and when the joking becomes too personal.

My own experience in Ireland included being slagged. During my time in Dublin, I met regularly—two or three times a week—with a group of friends who had known each other for many years. They slagged each other—and, eventually, me—good-naturedly. For instance, within three months of my arrival in Dublin, I cut my shoulder-length hair, changing my appearance rather drastically. I was a little nervous about this radical alteration and asked one of the group members if my hair looked all right the first time I ran into him. For the next year and a half, this man would say immediately upon meeting me, with a wicked twinkle in his eye, "Ah, your hair looks lovely." At first, I felt embarrassed to be teased in this way, but I soon realized that it was a marker of our friendship. This informant felt comfortable enough to knock me down a few pegs, regarding me as a intimate equal who shared his understanding that slagging was a marker of sociability between us. He also was subtly teaching me that concern over one's appearance was inappropriate and selfish; slagging was his educational tool.

A different interpretation of slagging is that it is a psychopathological, double-binding interaction. Scheper-Hughes, in her discussion of Kerry slagging, argues that escape from slagging is not possible (Scheper-Hughes 1979:183–185). She further does not believe that those on the receiving end of slagging (or "cracking," as she calls it) find the interaction amusing (Scheper-Hughes 1979:183). Because the recipients of the slag find it hurtful, but because they will be further slagged if they take offense, Scheper-Hughes says that Irish people are caught: they have to laugh at the public display of their personal pain, and this is paraschizophrenogenic communication, or double-binding. (Scheper-Hughes 1979:183–185). While Scheper-Hughes may be accurate in her analysis, my own observations and interpretations of slagging in 1990s Dublin, Waterford, and Limerick do not match those of Scheper-Hughes in deeply rural 1970s Kerry.

Slagging and the good-natured acceptance of potential insults is connected with Irish child-rearing practices. Irish parents tend to be businesslike, with an emphasis on physical nurturance and moral instruction, focusing on good temper and compliance. A mother fears raising a "bold" child, one who answers back, who wants more than his share, who expresses opinions, who appears greedy. One middle-aged man told me that he was raised never to be greedy: "If I was at me friend's house, me mother always told me, never take a biscuit [cookie] right away. The rule seemed to be that me friend's ma always had to ask me three times before I'd be sayin' yes. Yeh didn't want to look like yeh was greedy. Same with boastin'. Yeh never boast; that's greedy, too, like you're tryin' to show how much yeh have and how little the other one has." Teaching a child not to be greedy involves a series of activities; primarily, though, it requires the child to be submissive to authority and aware of others' needs and feelings.

This can be seen in adult interaction when a group of friends prepares to part company and leave the pub, coffee shop, or house. The unvarying question is asked by someone in the group, usually one of the more dominant members: "Will we go?" The required response is: "I don't mind." Informants, male and female, married and unmarried, young, middle-aged, and older, enacted this ritual uniformly; there was no variation whatsoever. When questioned about the ritual, all informants responded that it has to do with being polite; just because one person wants to go does not necessarily mean that everyone wants to go. "It's a way of getting everyone to agree, to close the evening out like," one middle-aged man said. Although a minor ritual, it is striking in that everyone performed it at the end of every event in which I participated. "Will we go?" and "I don't mind" indicate an Irish value on considering other people's wishes, feelings, and desires before one's own. It is in part a result of Irish child-rearing emphases on submission.

This submission can be interpreted several ways. For instance, Scheper-Hughes says, with some disapproval, that mothers will spoon-feed "even a four-year-old" because it is more efficient (Scheper-Hughes 1979:149). She goes on to interpret this as part of a set of child-rearing practices that rewards passivity, leading to damaging emotional denial (Scheper-Hughes 1979:160).[9] However, I observed similar behaviors among mothers and children in Dublin. For example, one mother in Dublin whom I came to know quite well would frequently button up her twelve-year-old boy's jacket when we went out. She would then fasten her eight-year-old boy's and six-year-old girl's garments as well. Although such behaviors conceivably could reward passivity and submission, they also make some sense. Buses come along only once in a while and, with so many children, it is indeed more efficient to have an adult dress the children than wait for pokey children to get themselves ready, possibly missing the bus. Dublin mothers, and fathers to a lesser extent, try to be efficient and instructive when dealing with their children. The American attention to self-esteem, creative expression, and nonjudgmental friendship in child rearing (Whiting and Edwards 1988: 113–117) does not obtain in Ireland; yet most children in fact grow up to be productive members of society.[10]

THE BUSINESS OF INTIMACY

Marriage—a goal for most Irish people—is, like child rearing, a rather businesslike proposition. Although I will explore marriage and the family in detail in later chapters, a brief discussion here is in order. Like other European peasant societies, marital relationships in Ireland remain outwardly fairly distant (compare Rogers's [1975] description of French marital relationships). Some younger couples are adopting a companionable relationship pattern, or what William Goode (1970) calls the "conjugal" family, rather than a child-centered or kin-based marriage. However, most of the families I knew in Dublin and other areas appeared to have a rather distant marital relationship. Spouses keep a good deal from each other; emotional intimacy and revelation are not prized elements of the relationship. Instead, most married couples I knew said they married for sex, a vaguely defined "love," and to have children.[11] While certainly it is hoped that they will like their partners, most Irish couples do not have a companionate marriage. At the same time, spouses discuss their day's activities, thoughts, and reactions to other people in somewhat more detail than they could within their kin and friendship networks. Irish husbands and wives do not reveal much of their emotional lives to each other, but they do share everyday sorrows and joys.

Deep emotional revelation is not a prized behavior in Ireland, either between spouses or between strangers. Very few feelings or even opinions are expressed "publicly"—that is, outside one's self. Unlike Scheper-Hughes (1979), however, I do not believe that this is a result of massive repression. My informants easily enough discussed their fears, hopes, dreams, and feelings with me, even if they do not with their spouses. This indicates not repression but suppression. If the emotions and thoughts are accessible—as they were with me—they are not repressed. Certainly Irish cultural norms discourage an overt display of deep emotion. Such a display would indicate a difference, in contravention of cultural emphases on leveling and equality (see Chapter 8). In addition, displays of emotion would be greedy, taking up other people's time, and they would, as one informant put it, "remind the other person of their own troubles." The Catholic Church, as well, does not encourage the intensive and independent self-analysis that deep emotional revelation requires, at least as I understand it within the framework of American psychotherapy in which I was trained as a social worker in the 1980s; for instance, the Church does not encourage intensive and independent intellectual analysis of its catechisms. In everyday social relations, whether marital, friendship, parental, or otherwise, Dubliners expect and enact an emotional distance. We turn now to a description of the city of Dublin, paying attention to the historical and physical environment of this "fair city."

NOTES

1. Taylor (1980; 1989a; 1989b; 1995) is the only anthropologist who attends to Ireland's colonial past. Irish sociologists Inglis (1987) and Dillon (1993) have analyzed colonialism in the context of Church and political issues. There are only a few psychological studies regarding the Irish experience of British colonialism; Moane (1994) is the most recent example. Most such psychological studies rely on Fanon (1967, 1968) and Memmi (1965) even though these authors discuss the African experience. The Irish experience of colonialism, I suspect, was likely significantly different. Clearly more analysis of this subject in terms of Ireland needs to be done.

2. I deal here only with the ethnography of the Republic of Ireland. Curtin et al. (1994) have provided a cogent summary of anthropological studies of Northern Ireland.

3. World Bank statistics show that, in the period 1988–1993, 57.3% of the Irish lived in urban areas, defined as towns or cities with populations of more than 1,500 (World Bank 1995:165).

4. There are no anthropological studies of which I am aware that compare contemporary urban life and rural life in the Republic, although Silverman and Gulliver (1992) have provided an historical anthropological approach, dealing with nineteenth-century Ireland. Ethnographic information regarding city and country cultural understandings has not been collated. This has led to an overemphasis on small, isolated communities, which are no longer the norm in Ireland.

5. In other modern societies, churches play significant roles as organizations that mediate between the government and the family—in other words, between the putatively public and the supposedly private spheres (Madsen, personal communication). In Ireland, however, as has been seen, the Catholic Church has acted in concert with the government until very recently. This means that the Church has been less of an intermediary influence in Ireland than in other modern societies. Additionally, Catholic organizations that are

ostensibly independent from the Hierarchy have been shown to be under the Hierarchy's control. Opus Dei, the Knights of St. Columbanus, the Society for the Protection of the Unborn Child, Family Solidarity, and the Legion of Mary have played significant roles in influencing legislation of interest to the Church (O'Reilly 1992). O'Reilly has demonstrated that, rather than acting as separate and independent lobbyists or intermediary organizations, these groups merely have appeared to be individual political action groups. Truly intermediary organizations in Ireland consist of sports, musical, dancing, or social clubs. Sporting clubs very often are overseen by the local parish priest, however, and their intermediary nature is unclear.

6. Dennis Gaffin describes similar joking relationships in the Faeroe Islands (Gaffin 1995).

7. Teasing is an important part of Irish child rearing, as Scheper-Hughes has shown (Scheper-Hughes 1979:153). Slagging may be the adult elaboration of teasing.

8. If one tries to slag someone who is not well-known, the slag will be taken as an insult. One way to prevent inappropriate slagging is to describe oneself in deprecatory terms, in effect insulting oneself before anyone else can do so.

9. It should be remembered that Scheper-Hughes's study was based on incorrect assumptions regarding the rates of Irish schizophrenia. At the time of her research, schizophrenia incidence rates were approximately 1%, not 6% as she claims. Psychiatrists and Irish social scientists, in concurrent research published in 1990 (Ni Nuallain et al. 1990), demonstrated this. Scheper-Hughes's contention, then, that her descriptions of schizophrenogenic child-rearing practices explained the high schizophrenia rate (Scheper-Hughes 1979:160), despite the fact that most of the people she observed were not schizophrenic, is questionable.

10. Scheper-Hughes (1979) has an implicit and strongly middle-class American outlook with which she assesses the Irish. Throughout her book, Scheper-Hughes seems to believe that children should be raised to be emotionally expressive, independent, opinionated, and generally free. Because the Irish have different goals, Scheper-Hughes criticizes them, despite the very real fact that most Irish children and adults, like most people everywhere, get on just fine. The Irish are no more pathological than Americans; given our divorce and crime rates, I wonder whether we are in fact more pathological than the Irish Scheper-Hughes condemns.

11. Results of a questionnaire administered during fieldwork bear this out. Of 133 respondents, 88 said that "love" was the primary reason for marriage. Other significant answers were companionship (59), to start a family (58), security (48), and societal expectations (41). (Numbers add up to more than 133 because respondents were encouraged to list several reasons for marriage.)

CHAPTER 4

Net Curtains and Back Gardens: Dublin c. 1994

The ancient city of Dublin, and its suburbs, comprise a 1994 population of 1.5 million people, one-third of the entire Irish population. It is, by any standards, a city. But it is an Irish city. Blending anonymous city interaction familiar to urban dwellers everywhere and a voluble Irish sociability, Dublin is a city marked by anonymous friendliness and distant friendships that show Irish understandings and experience of publicness and privateness. The well-settled neighborhoods, the semi-detached houses, the net curtains, the small shops, the intimate pubs and restaurants, and the narrow streets all reflect Dublin's face-to-face interactional style in the midst of crowds and strangers. In this chapter, I briefly describe Dublin's history and the neighborhoods in which I worked so that later discussions of Irish social life, the blending of aspects of Irish public and private life, may be placed in social and physical context. Before walking through the streets of Dublin, however, I provide a brief note on culture and material items.

MATERIAL ITEMS AND CULTURE

In this chapter, I describe the neighborhood—actually a composite of several areas, which I call Rathkelly—in which I worked. Such a description is important if one is to understand the total environment of the Dubliners I discuss in later chapters. Homes are not in themselves culture; they are neither public nor private. Although some anthropologists argue that "material culture" is most important in understanding (Harris 1979) or "interpreting" human behavior (e.g., Siegel 1981), an analyst's treatment of physical environment or maps of the physical environment is not description or analysis of culture. Rather, houses, roads, buildings, interior and exterior furnishings, and even maps are physical embodiments of cultural understandings. Such implements and structures are the result of culture. They are not in and of themselves culture. Cognitive–emotional understandings containing information needed to build houses, to make furniture, to hang wallpaper, to lay carpet, to cover windows with net curtains, are culture. The items themselves are not. In this study, the emphasis is on people and their cultural understandings, and not on their physical environment. Still, some context is illuminating; the ubiquitous net curtains, material items, in Ireland are used by Irish people in specifically Irish ways, as will be discussed later in this chapter.

Net curtains, though specifically Irish,[1] are not Irish culture. The cultural understandings that frame the reasons, motivations, thoughts, and consequences regarding hanging, washing, or twitching net curtains are. These understandings are cognitive–emotional, incompletely shared but still shared, and, in this instance, given the pervasive window coverings, widely shared in Irish culture. Net curtains are a splendid metaphor for Irish cultural understandings regarding privacy. You can see out, you can observe, but you can't be seen, you can't be observed.

Issues of public and private understandings in Ireland will be explored in depth in the following chapters. In this chapter, I discuss the physical environment in which some of the cultural understandings are used by Irish people. As will be seen, the Dublin physical environment provides opportunities for Irish people to enact and experience cultural understandings regarding privacy, family life, adulthood, and reputation.

VIKINGS, ANGLO-NORMANS, AND THE BRITISH: DUBLIN'S HISTORY

Dubliners take great pride in their city's antiquity. Although there is some scanty evidence that Dublin was a village prior to Danish-Norse (Viking) invasion in the ninth century (Gwynn 1938:6; Graham 1993: 38–39), archaeological evidence shows that the Vikings developed and walled the settlement after briefly abandoning it in 902 A.D. (Graham 1993:39). Much of the City Centre owes its layout to Viking urban planning, as excavations that were taking place when I lived in Dublin showed. Centered on the banks of the River Liffey, which runs through the middle of Dublin's City Centre, the Viking settlement was fortified with thick stone walls. These walls were visible after laborious digging by Irish archaeologists in the mid-1990s; some of those archaeologists, with whom I had struck up friendships, showed me the walls imbedded in the basements in current commercial establishments.

The Vikings appear to have permanently settled in Ireland, intermarrying with the indigenous Irish, unlike most of their British successors. This did not save them, however, from the wrath of Irish kings, who demanded and finally took control, after bloody battles, of Dublin and the other smaller cities that the Vikings established (Waterford, Wexford, Limerick, and Cork) (Graham 1993:39). Irish kings apparently saw the value in having a centralized and well-defended capital city, and Dublin was it (Graham 1993:41).

Like other parts of Ireland, Dublin in the eleventh and twelfth centuries was in the grip of constant battling between various Irish kings, one gaining control of the city for a few years and then losing to another (Simms 1986:53). As noted in Chapter 2, it was in fact the Irish who invited the British government, in the form of the Anglo-Normans, to Ireland to assist in settling internal wars between kings (Graham 1993: 62). It was, however, the Anglo-Normans who ultimately seized power, and Dublin.

Authority was almost immediately centered in Dublin. Anglo-Norman, and later British, centralized governmental structures were located in this eastern port. B. J. Graham, a historical geographer, remarks that the eastern parts of the island were the first to be colonized, although the instability of the Irish kingships allowed some Anglo-Normans to invade and seize other territories with impunity (Graham 1993:63). Dublin and its Pale remained firmly in Anglo-Norman, British hands from the eleventh century until the twentieth.

REMNANTS OF EARLIER SETTLEMENT

Even in the twentieth century, Viking and Anglo-Norman/British settlement patterns can be seen in Dublin's physical structures. As in so many ancient cities, roads in Dublin, particularly in the City Centre, are barely wide enough for one automobile to pass through. That does not constrict motor traffic in the capital city, however. Despite the fact that roads were designed for foot and horse or ass-cart traffic, Dublin drivers cheerfully and sometimes recklessly careen through streets not quite six feet wide. Pedestrians, however, are rarely struck by oncoming traffic, watching carefully for the "green man," a pedestrian traffic signal that signals that it is safe to cross the road. The few horse or ass carts that still travel through the city, usually delivering turf (peat, a form of fuel burned in fireplaces) or coal, tend to be accident free as well, perhaps because drivers take care to avoid them as much as possible.

One can see a good many carts powered by real horsepower traveling through the Liberties, a poverty-stricken area[2] on the south side of the city behind the Guinness Brewery in the City Centre. The Liberties is a neighborhood of narrow streets that ultimately lead up to Christ Church Cathedral, perhaps the oldest church structure still in use in Ireland (Gwynn 1938:9). Two-story, and sometimes three-story, red brick or gray stone flats and houses line the streets between and above the innumerable small storefronts selling wares ranging from freshly plucked poultry to Communion dresses and suits. All is cement, bricks, asphalt, and litter, and little sunlight makes its way to the footpaths and windows of the Liberties. At the same time, it is a lively and energetic place. Still, it is, as one of my informants told me, "a desperate place altogether." Since the early 1700s, the Liberties has been one of the poorest[3] tenement areas of Dublin (O'Brien 1982:9–10). Indeed, I was told that it is in the Liberties that extensive drug dealing and criminal activity persists; it has been a center of illicit and bloody dealings almost from its inception. So, for instance, in 1994 on Hallowe'en, a usually boisterous and violent night in Dublin, in the Liberties, and in Clondalkin, a western suburb, informants living in the Liberties, and the Irish electronic media, reported that people were shot, bonfires of tires and rags soaked in gasoline raged out of control, and a small riot ensued when the Garda arrived. Almost all other neighborhoods were quiet.

The Liberties is, perhaps, an extreme example of the poverty of Dublin. Although the Liberties is on the south side of the city, it is as dangerous, if not more, as the more notorious north side of the city.

A TALE OF TWO CITIES

Dubliners, somewhat inaccurately, identify the north side of the city as working-class, and the south side as the middle-class and upper-middle class area. The River Liffey bisects the City Centre, effectively dividing crowded, dirty O'Connell Street on the north from the more pristine, pedestrian-friendly Grafton Street on the south. Grafton Street houses the more upscale shops—Switzer's and Brown-Thomas department stores, A-Wear, Hodges Figgis and Waterstone's Books, Stephen's Green shopping centre. O'Connell Street contains shops selling more reasonably priced goods—Penney's department store, Eason's Stationery and Books, the ILAC shopping centre. Both Grafton Street and O'Connell Street have McDonald's restaurants; apparently Big

Mac Attacks afflict the moneyed and the penniless alike. Grafton Street is a pedestrian mall, with vehicular traffic prohibited from 10 A.M. until the late evening. O'Connell Street, on the other hand, is a six-lane road, usually choked with automobile, lorry, and bus traffic throughout the day. A pedestrian takes her life into her hands crossing O'Connell Street even when the "green man" is flashing "walk now"; one never knows when a capricious driver may decide to take a sudden left turn directly into the crosswalk.

O'Connell Street and Grafton Street reflect the two divided worlds in Dublin. One is a gritty working-class world, relatively unprotected from metaphorical capricious drivers. My working-class informants were builders, shop clerks, factory workers, or, as they themselves said, would be working class if they were working;[4] often they were on "the dole" (social welfare grants) and subject to social welfare intervention usually avoided by the middle class. The other world is more genteel, more impregnable. The middle class, however, is only a step away from O'Connell Street: most middle-class people I knew came from working-class Dublin families (contra Humphreys 1966). More rarely, they may have been raised in farming families "down the country." Rising to schoolteacher or civil service posts—office or professional jobs—seemed to mark the middle class from the working class for Dubliners.

Occupational position is not the only salient marker of class position. Neighborhoods are significant as well. However, geographical position on the north or south side of the river, as seen above in the description of the Liberties, does not always predict class position. On the north side, for example, Clontarf, Dollymount, and Howth are middle-class, well-settled areas, and Phibsborough, though a mixed neighborhood, attracts young single professionals as well as working-class families. And the south side, though containing the middle-class and upper-middle-class neighborhoods of Rathgar, Rathfarnham, Ranelagh, Ballsbridge, Clonskeagh, Sandymount, and Templelogue, has its share of sometimes difficult and clearly working-class areas: Drimnagh, Crumlin, Ballyfermot, Inchicore, Harold's Cross, Kimmage, and Dolphin's Barn.

Middle-class areas, north or south, have trees, very well-tended front gardens, clean and wide streets, and few flats, terraced houses, or row houses. There is little foot traffic, shops are quite a distance away (requiring a drive, and thus a car, rather than a walk), and one sees block after block of houses. Few commercial concerns are sited nearby. As in so many middle-class neighborhoods across the world, Irish middle-class neighborhoods are bastions of calm, privacy, and civility. One might twitch the net curtains to see comings and goings more clearly, but one would rarely comment on daily activities outside the home.

However, many of the physical and behavioral patterns that obtain in Dublin's middle-class neighborhoods apply to working-class areas as well. The ubiquitous net curtains—filmy, lacy white curtains hung either from the top or the middle of a window—cover almost all Dublin window glass. They are twitched with interest across class. The middle class attempts to be less obvious; it tries to adhere to more rigid standards of privacy in that obvious observation does not take place in the way it does in working-class areas. Still, net curtains and close neighbors persist regardless of class.

A typical Dublin house, whether working-class or middle-class, is semidetached.[5] That is, it is either a duplex (two residences sharing a common middle wall) or a row or terraced house (one of up to eight [or more] residences sharing common walls with immediate neighbors). Even in the suburbs, where, presumably, there is a bit more room, most houses are semidetached. One must have a great deal of money to have a detached home. In fact, in one far-flung, wealthy western suburb I visited, there was a row of semidetached cottages surrounded by wasteland. Despite the availability of cheap land, zoning officials and developers apparently elected to build semidetached homes in this place. This in part reflects an Irish cultural understanding about how one should place oneself geographically—that is, people ought to live near each other and not in isolation. This is a physical marker of Irish cultural understandings regarding privacy, intimacy, and isolation.[6]

Except in very rural areas, most people seem to live in semidetached houses. Even in rural areas, there are close groupings of cottages. Unlike, for example, communities with which I am familiar in rural parts of the Midwest, houses do not sit in splendid isolation. If there is a possibility of siting houses near each other in rural Ireland, that opportunity has been taken, a physical exemplar, in part, of Irish cultural understandings regarding sociability. Customs regarding neighborliness, appropriate levels of interest in neighbors' activities, and ability to observe such activities are discouraged by single-family detached homes.

It is not possible to hear, for example, rows from the family next door if a family lives in a single-family detached home, unless the family is particularly loud, unlike families living in semidetached homes. Informants living in a working-class area of south Dublin frequently reported activities—usually loud and sometimes violent fights—of their common-wall neighbors. My informants could hear their neighbors well enough. At times, the family wondered whether they should be ringing the Garda Siochana (the police, also called the "guards"). At one point, given the escalation of violence, the wife in this informant family called over after the violent husband next door had left for the pub. She advised the female neighbor to find shelter elsewhere and offered to help find the neighbor find another place. The offer was refused politely, and the Guards were never called, though the informant husband stepped in a few times. After one instance, the informant husband counseled the violent husband a day or two after the incident, advising the violent husband to stop drinking. The violent family was living together when I left the field.

This kind of intervention does not indicate, however, a drastic difference in cultural understandings between working-class and middle-class, or north side and south side, understandings. Neighbors can hear each other in most parts of Dublin. Inhabitants of middle-class and working-class areas will notice families who row and families who do not, hoping, of course, for the latter. In both cases—rowing and non-rowing families—and in both classes—middle-class and working-class—it is unlikely that the Garda will be called in.

Neighbors rarely interfere directly or indirectly with the activities of adults, although in some areas adults will correct children. One man, living in a working-class area on the south side of the city, watches children playing on the road outside his home. If play becomes too rough, or if a fight breaks out, "Joe" intervenes almost immediately. He described one incident, which he said was typical, in which two young lads, about twelve years old, began fistfighting. Joe noticed the row and burst out his front door with some concern. The lads were fighting in the middle of the road—there was no automobile traffic—and they were beating each other severely. As Joe reached the pair, a door opened directly across from Joe's, and another man came out. Both Joe and his neighbor took a lad by the collar and physically separated them, none too gently, by Joe's description. The two men roared at the lads, telling them that such behavior was desperate and disgraceful, and did they want to be marched right away so that the men could have a talk with the mammies (the boys' mothers)? The boys both shook their heads vehemently and, at the adults' instruction, shook hands and scampered away in opposite directions. Joe is proud of his intervention. He sees it as important to maintaining a sense of "community" (his term) in the middle of a poor housing estate.

RATHKELLY—INSIDE AND OUT

Joe and his family, and many of the families with whom I worked, live in "Rathkelly,"[7] a working-class neighborhood on Dublin's south side. Rathkelly and adjacent working-class areas are clustered in the south and southwestern center of Dublin. Although considered by many inhabitants to be suburbs, in fact legally the neighborhoods belong to Dublin City. In addition, working-class areas are concentrated in the central south side of Dublin, while the north side working-class population is more dispersed throughout the north side despite its reputation as almost entirely working-class. Rathkelly and its neighbors flow into one another, stopped more or less on the northwest side by the River Liffey, on the northeasterly side (though more diffusely) by the Grand Canal and on the south by the River Dodder and more upscale neighborhoods, containing flats, apartments, and a few large detached homes in addition to terraced or semidetached houses, such as Rathmines, Ranelagh, and Rathgar.

Rathkelly and its neighbors have a different feel to them than the upscale or middle-class family areas. Although for the most part the feel is ineffable and diffuse, some differences can be described. Unlike the middle-class or upscale areas, trees of any appreciable size, shrubbery, front gardens, and lawns are literally thin on the ground. The lack of foliage contributes to a sense of desolation in these working-class areas. Much of Rathkelly consists of concrete and brick. One set of schoolyards with which I became familiar is entirely paved over and surrounded by eight-foot wrought-iron fences, to keep drug dealers and vandals out and children in, away from a busy road. The one small patch of green space is centered around the convent serving the schools.

At the same time, there is one circular park in the area, which appears to be seldom used. It provides the only shrubbery and lawn of any size in the neighborhood. It also adds to the desolation of the neighborhood, as it has neither trees nor flowers and at times—particularly at night—I found it downright menacing, particularly after informants warned me to steer clear of the park after dark. The park does relieve the density of the neighborhood, however, as six to eight semidetached houses could have been built there without difficulty.

All of Rathkelly and other south-side working-class neighborhoods consist of semidetached privately owned[8] houses, which contain two residences that share a common middle wall, with deep but narrow lots. All of the houses are built to the same basic plan: two bedrooms upstairs, a small downstairs front room, and a back room/kitchen, less than 900 square feet in all. Over the years, owners have improved their houses in various ways. For example, one family I knew bought a house in the 1980s; the previous owner had installed an indoor bathroom just a few years ago and had used a privy in the backyard before that. My informants had built an eat-in kitchen addition to the back of the house, replacing a galley kitchen that had been placed against the side wall of what is now their back sitting room. They also added a modified central heating system, with vents in the back sitting room and the upstairs hallway but not in the kitchen or the bedrooms. Completely central heating is still fairly rare in Irish housing because of the installation expense and the cost of energy in Ireland;[9] heating only a few rooms and keeping doors of other rooms tightly closed reduces the cost of heating. Oftentimes, in fact, the heat is turned off for most of the day and only used in the evenings before bed. This family's improvements are not unusual in Rathkelly. Like so many of their neighbors, this family has improved the inside of their house but has neglected, for the most part, the outside appearance of their house except to keep it more or less neat (see Ardagh 1994:155–156 for a brief discussion of the lack of "visual sense," as he calls it, among the Irish). Though some owners have attempted to spruce up the outside of their homes, for the most part it is difficult to differentiate one house from another.

In Rathkelly, the exteriors of most houses are plain. The front garden area consists of either a very small, poorly tended lawn or a paved driveway. The more daring householder has attached a pebbledash or multicolored asphalt brick facing to the front of the house; the more pious one may have a small grotto devoted to Our Lady or the Sacred Heart. In the main, however, home owners have not altered the street-facing exteriors, which consist of a sprayed gray or off-white stucco. There is little diversity in color among the homes of Rathkelly.

Almost all windows, front and back, downstairs and upstairs, in Rathkelly—as indeed in almost every home in Ireland in which I sat— are swathed in white net curtains, shadowed with heavy floor-to-ceiling drapes. Net curtains allow a person to observe activities taking place outside without being noticed: you can see out but you cannot see in, regardless of whether the curtains are half-length, covering the lower half of the window, or full-length. These curtains are never drawn open but hang suspended over the entire width of the window. The curtains also are usually snow-white, as housewives take pains to keep the interior of their house "looking well." A wife will be criticized—behind her back, usually—by other women if she does not keep her curtains, and her windows, sparkling clean. Net curtains provide another marker of uniformity to the passerby.

Passersby do not see back gardens, and it is in these that more physical diversity can be seen. Back gardens are almost always divided by high gray stone walls from adjacent gardens, but the walls are often the only sign of commonality. In Rathkelly, the stone walls are high enough to inhibit neighborly chat, generally six to seven feet high. Many people get past this by placing wooden crates or paving stones next to the wall, so that they can chat with neighbors. The walls do not inhibit criminal activity, however: one informant related with great relish the story of a burglar who was chased over the tops of the stone walls in the neighborhood, finally being tripped up by a quick-thinking neighbor with a strong stick placed strategically in the burglar's direct path. Still, for the most part, the walls allow Dubliners to avoid chat and crime if they wish; a sociable neighbor must make quite an effort to get the attention of, much less an invitation from, the people next door.

Rathkelly's walls may be more or less uniform, but the interiors of back gardens are not. Some back gardens are very well tended, with carefully watered and pruned vegetable and flower patches, the ubiquitous clothes lines, small lawns, even smaller flagstone patios, sometimes domestic animals such as chickens or geese or even a horse, and the occasional back shed containing tools and garden implements. Many, though by no means all, gardens contain religious statuary of some kind, most often statues of Mary, Jesus, or various saints. Less often will a back garden be entirely disused, and such a slovenly householder will be regarded with little favor by his neighbors. Neglect of a back garden for many inhabitants of Rathkelly means that the householder is involved in criminal activities of one kind or another—drug dealing, robberies, drug use, or taking on too many "nixers" (jobs paid in cash and therefore not taxed[10])—or is just plain lazy. Back gardens, marking out more "private" space for a family, are still very much public, and most householders are aware of this. A family's reputation among immediate neighbors is partly made by the condition of the back garden.

Within Rathkelly, through choices of wallpaper and sitting-room "suites," interiors appear to be even more variable than back gardens. In actuality, however, Rathkelly—and Irish interiors in general—are, like exteriors, fairly uniform. Though primary colors may differ, most sitting rooms contain this basic grouping: a settee or sofa, two or three armchairs that may or may not match the settee, a coffee table placed either in front of the settee or sofa or one of the armchairs, and small occasional tables. If table lamps are present, which is seldom, they contain low-wattage bulbs. On the whole, ceiling lights and the telly (television) are used as lighting sources. Wallpaper is the usual choice of wallcovering, and it is unusual to see bare painted walls in sitting rooms and indeed in most rooms of a Rathkelly house.

A typical sitting room, the usual meeting place of families, is oblong. Perhaps twelve feet long, it is at most nine feet wide and eight feet high. The heavy furniture favored by most informants includes the settees or sofas and armchairs mentioned above, usually covered by dark red, green, or blue velvet, velveteen, or heavy cotton-polyester blends and punctuated by thick matching upholstery buttons. Every once in a while, informant homes would sport patterned sofas, typically in a brown plaid pattern or a subtle striped pattern, usually a primary color with tiny white stripes. On the whole, however, unless the family is desperately poor (and thus relying on cast-offs), the sofa would be a uniform, well-tended color with thick arms and legs and boasting often wildly contrasting occasional pillows and throws.

Sometimes furniture and wallpaper match; sometimes they do not. Sometimes they clash in interesting but ultimately harmonious and unanticipated ways. One family with whom I often visited had a sitting-room suite that was overwhelmingly, and not unpleasantly, blue; their wallpaper was a nicely contrasting floral and striped brownish-green. Halfway through my fieldwork, the family repapered, so that the stripes and the flowers were pink and brown rather than green. The pink worked better in this small sitting room, to my untrained interior decorator's eye.

Most sitting rooms, and most rooms in general, in Rathkelly and in Ireland, are closed off by doors. Unlike the more open plan of most American houses, rooms are marked by closed doors; free and easy movement between rooms is not possible, though the doors are rarely locked. Air flow and heat dissipation are inhibited as well, important given energy costs. Conversations cannot take place through closed doors. Consequently, interaction is affected in oblique ways, though of course not determined by, the physical structure of the house. Despite the fact that closed doors could be interpreted as affording privacy, in reality one is always aware that there are others around. Doors do not keep people out or privacy in, really. One expects that a door will be opened at any time; a call while opening the door, rather than a knock, is an appropriately polite way of interrupting the occupant.

Although Rathkelly's housing is slightly more dispersed than that in the inner city, Rathkelly has a high population density, consisting mainly of families that have lived in the area for quite some time. Rathkelly's uniformly small two-bedroom houses were, in the main, built after World War II. Informants told me that the area was a planned public housing estate when the Irish government began slum and tenement clearance of the inner city in the late 1940s. At first, Rathkelly and other areas were rough areas, as inhabitants had difficulties adjusting to the more isolated life of the "suburbs" after the closeness of inner-city living. However, as the first wave of inhabitants raised families and grew older, the area settled down and became solidly working-class rather than solely poverty-stricken as it had been at inception. In 1994, Rathkelly, like many urban areas, had its share of problems, consisting mainly of overt drug dealing and burglary, but it also has a nascent community spirit developing through organized "neighborhood watch" programs and growing parental involvement in primary school affairs.[11]

TRIPS THROUGH RATHKELLY

To get to informants' homes in Rathkelly, I traveled by Dublin Bus or walked from my flat in a neighboring area. Here I describe two such trips and the broad outlines of these visits, typical for most of my journeys in and out of Rathkelly. These trips provide not only a word picture of Dublin, but also show interactions that contain almost exclusively public elements. Since I "passed" for Irish in interactions that were nearly completely public, my experiences paralleled those of Dubliners.

One absolutely dreadful night in January 1995, the sleet and the rain were lashing down in buckets. Though Ireland, and Dublin, is normally very rainy and windy in the winter, a gale rose this freezing night. Raindrops, hail, sleet, and snow were whipped around in the cruelly cold wind, making my large black umbrella superfluous if not sometimes dangerously airborne in the gale. I made my way through Ranelagh to the bus stop some five blocks, leaving my warm and cozy flat to battle this freezing monsoon. Winters in Dublin can pack nearly hurricane-force winds, bringing down power lines, flooding streets quickly, and rattling windows to a frightening extent. This was one such storm.

Just before this particular bus stop, contained in a narrow sidewalk not more than three feet wide outside a small newsagent's, buses make a wide turn from busy Ranelagh Road into the "Triangle," a T-intersection at Ranelagh Road and Charleston Road. One does not know whether a bus is approaching until it is almost at the stop. Opening an umbrella at the tiny bus stop effectively closes off foot traffic and so my umbrella, useless anyway in the driving rain, remained closed. After 20 minutes, a bus finally arrived; I greeted it with relief and with water running down my waxed jacket and into my shoes. Buses in Dublin come in two styles: they are either rather rickety bright green double-deckers or newer single-deckers built to EU standards. The bus this night was the latter type, to my relief. The EU buses have powerful heating systems and, more importantly, do not leak, unlike the older double-deckers. The bus driver, despite being ensconced behind bulletproof and potentially soundproof Plexiglas on this sometimes dangerous route, took my fare with a smile and a rueful comment about the dreadful weather.

Such interaction is not unusual.[12] There is a clear set of understandings regarding proper sociable bus behavior, the primary one being that a passenger must chat with the driver when embarking or disembarking. Although in general passengers do not chat unless they know each other, almost every passenger says "hello" or "how're yez?" to the driver as either a ten-day computerized bus ticket or a special bus pass is used, or a fare is paid. The driver almost always says at least "how're yez?"

in response, and often he will remark on the weather or the traffic. Once the bus is traveling, however, the driver does not talk except to his conductor[13] if one is present—given the challenge of Dublin traffic, this is a good thing indeed. One signals one's stop by pressing a red button located in various parts of the bus and usually a passenger should move to the front of the bus unless it is quite crowded. As in boarding, upon disembarking a passenger should speak to the driver. A "good luck" or "thanks a million" or "safe home now" will be offered by the driver if the passenger does not speak; this is a signal for the passenger to be properly sociable and mark her departure. Such interaction is an example of a role relationship with primarily public dimensions.

On this stormy night, the driver's anonymous friendliness was welcome. I chose a seat toward the front and arranged myself and my umbrella so that I dripped mainly on the floor and little on my already-wet clothing. The trip to Rathkelly, which normally took 15 minutes, took a half-hour in the downpour and the winds despite the paucity of passengers and concomitant stops. The weather also made discerning location difficult, as the cold and the damp, meeting the heating system of the bus, fogged up the bus windows completely. I rose, somewhat earlier than necessary, when the number of turns the bus made felt "right." I was off by a few blocks, but the driver was patient with my confusion: "Yeh can't see a t'ing out at all now. Where're yeh off?" I told him. When we reached my stop, he carefully steered the bus to the curb so that I could avoid the flooding street. I thanked him, receiving in response, "Safe home now in th'storm!"

The bus stop nearest the home of the family whom I was visiting this night is a six-block walk. It is also located in an abnormally windy area of Rathkelly: the combination of wide roads and nearby school grounds somehow conspire to make this area a veritable wind tunnel. Umbrellas on a normal Dublin day are difficult to use here. On this night, I considered it potentially lethal to open my umbrella—the wind, gusting (so I learned later) to 50 m.p.h., would have snatched the umbrella, and perhaps my arm, violently away. Instead, I brought the hood of my waxed jacket far forward, tying it tightly under my neck. I was immediately drenched.

Fighting my way across the "wind-tunnel" road, I was nearly blown down; luckily, no traffic dared travel on this night. Once I reached the relative safety of the other side of the road, the winds died a bit, cut off by the semidetached houses. The roads in this part of Rathkelly are wider than most Dublin streets, accommodating full parking on both sides of the street—rather than the usual Dublin practice of putting two wheels of a car on a footpath (sidewalk)—and two wide lanes of traffic. Despite their width, these streets do not act as wind conductors in the way the bus stop road does. On this night, the wind needed no encouragement and continued to bluster around me, pushing me this way and that across the wide footpaths. Normally I would reach this family's house in five minutes. It took me three times as long as I fought the gale.

I met no one on the street. There were usually teenagers chatting, smoking, and, I suspect, occasionally drinking on the low walls enclosing some of the front gardens in Rathkelly. Though they looked surly to my eyes, these young people were often helpful and friendly in responding to adult inquiries. Not surprisingly, they were not out this night. Neither were the drug dealers I had been told about. I finally arrived drenched and freezing at the house. I rang the bell and was met with a surprised face. "I didn't expect yeh to come out in this weather. We was expecting you to ring to cancel; the weather's dreadful!" said the wife. I replied, "Ah, this is a bad time . . . I can come back . . ." and, having learned at least one aspect of the subtle Irish communication style, looked despairingly out at the rain. "Don't be silly, of course it isn't. Come in and dry off. We'll get a cup o'tea in yeh."

Rathkelly, then, is marked by rain, wind, and cold, as is most of Dublin for most of the year. Temperatures, from my observation, rarely fell below 30° F on winter nights, usually rising to the low to mid 40s during the day. In the summer, lows averaged around 55° F and highs were generally around 68; it was unusual, and uncomfortable, for temperatures to rise above 75. Wind and rain are ever-present, made tolerable by higher temperatures in the spring, summer, and autumn. An entirely clear day is rare either in winter or summer.

The day before the Rathkelly gale described above I traveled to an informant's house located on the far edges of the neighborhood. In contrast to both the rain and the housing estate, this trip was made in a sunny afternoon, though with a stiff, cold north breeze. Rather than taking the bus—since none goes near this particular house directly—I walked from my flat in Ranelagh along the Grand Canal. While the Canal very likely tunneled the breeze, making it stronger to some extent, the walk along the Canal was pleasant enough.

I left my flat walking through Ranelagh village to the Canal and turned north, taking thirty minutes to get to my informant's house. The road running parallel to the Canal is well traveled in terms of both pedestrian and auto traffic, at least through Rathmines. The segment of the road straddling Ranelagh and Rathmines contains three-story Georgian houses set well back from the street, sometimes with private roads that occasionally dip five feet below street level. Most of the houses remain private residences, though some are being converted to flats. Few have front gardens or lawns of any appreciable size, though large deciduous trees and tall, well-tended shrubbery are commonplace. The fronts of most of these gray-faced houses are instead taken up with wide, tall sets of steps that provide access to the first, rather than the ground, floor.

Once Rathmines is passed, buildings become more mixed. The Georgian homes are absent, replaced by newer and older commercial office buildings, terraced houses, and the Cathal Brugha Barracks (police headquarters). Pubs are present as well, close to intersections. There are no shops of any kind along the road, though, like the pubs, some appear near busy crossroads. On the other side of the Canal, and the road, sits Portobello College, a third-level technical institution that offers instruction in secretarial skills and other technical subjects for postsecondary students. North of Portobello are minuscule one-story terraced houses with no gardens, sitting flush with the road and each other.

Upon reaching Harold's Cross Road, pubs and shops are in easy reach, serving a large purpose-built office complex as well as the neighborhood. The area on the other side of the Canal, however, is a bit more dicey and industrial: a coalmonger's yard takes up a good deal of untidy space. Past this commercial area, houses reassert themselves on the road side of the Canal until Kilmainham is reached. A large low-rise public housing estate is sited on the other side of the Canal, and two ten-story public housing buildings are nearby as well.

Walking the Canal Road—which has several different names as it follows the Canal—is often a pleasant, if bracing, experience. Winds whip down from the north with ferocity, stirring up litter and dust. Heavy auto and lorry traffic assist in this. One often meets fellow travelers as they come from the shops or walk down the footpath. The etiquette of street chat is one of the more extreme examples of very public interaction in Dublin, and it is age-graded. Older people, men or women, will say hello, at least to other adults; men who are wearing hats or caps will tip them. A quick comment on the weather may be had. If people know each other, they may stand and chat for quite some time. Younger people, however, rarely acknowledge passersby, although younger women will say hello to other women more readily than younger men will speak to anyone.

On this particular day, I walked this route, meeting a number of people, most of whom nodded and some of whom offered a comment on the cold breeze. Almost all passersby were OAPs, old-age pensioners. The few young men whom I met did not look up from the ground. Young women, and girls, glanced up quickly and looked away, a few with a brief smile. The interaction of strangers on the Canal Road is, however, different from that in areas with heavier foot traffic. In Ranelagh, the busy neighborhood where I lived for close to a year, the volume of passersby seemed to inhibit acknowledgment of others. The Canal Road, in contrast, has less foot traffic and thus might make it easier to be more sociable. One cannot ignore or neglect to notice that someone is approaching on the Canal Road; in Ranelagh and other village centers in Dublin there are so many people that acknowledgment is not, apparently, required. It is in the Canal Road.

General and specific examples of Dublin's history and what Dublin looks like have been provided in this chapter. Semidetached houses and front gardens looking very much alike, back gardens with more variety, net curtains, and interior decoration have been discussed as reflections of Irish cultural understandings regarding what is public and what is private. Interaction on the streets of Rathkelly has also been briefly discussed, again within the context of public and private. This discussion of Dublin in the 1990s has been in the service of orientation, so that the deeper analysis of social relations in Dublin can be placed in a physical context. Next, in Chapter 5, I present an overview of some of the role relationships involved in Dublin social life.

NOTES

1. Net curtains also appear in English and European windows, though to a lesser extent than the near-universal Irish window covering.

2. The official poverty line in 1987 was IR £48 a week, approximately US$72 (Daly 1989:5). The average weekly gross wage in 1987 for Irish men was IR£232.45 (US$348.68); for Irish women, it was IR£139.89 (US$209.83). The discrepancy in male and female wages is due in part to the fact that women frequently hold part-time rather than full-time jobs (Daly 1989:42–43). Adult women held 78% of all available part-time jobs in 1987, while adult men held only 2% of those jobs (Daly 1989:46).

3. Although no figures are available to me that were calculated after 1975, the Irish distribution of wealth then was as follows: the top 20% of households held 39% of the wealth; the bottom 40% held 20%; and the bottom 20% held 7% (World Bank 1995:165).

4. Recall that Ireland has an unemployment rate of 17%; in poor neighborhoods or suburbs it can reach 70% (Family Matters, RTE, February 9, 1994). Unemployment rates have slightly decreased in the 1980s: the number of registered unemployed was 19.1% in 1987, 18.6% in 1988, and 17.8% in 1989 (*European Communities Encyclopedia and Directory* 1992:141). My informants tell me that by 1998 the official rate is about 13%.

5. The current average purchase price of a small house was estimated to be IR £50,000 (Irish Consulate, Chicago, personal communication); this is approximately US$80,000. Total household expenses increased 21% from 1980 to 1986 in Ireland, while the EC average increase was 15% (*European Communities Encyclopedia and Directory* 1992:192–193). The average hourly Irish wage, calculated in US$, was $3.03 in 1975 and $12.18 in 1993; in comparison, the U.S. average hourly rate was $6.36 in 1975 and $16.73 in 1993, while in

the United Kingdom it was $3.37 and $12.76, respectively (*World Almanac* 1996:152). The lowest hourly wage recorded among the selected countries was in Sri Lanka, in which the 1975 hourly wage was $0.28 and the 1993 wage was $0.42 (*World Almanac* 1996:152).

6. This can be seen in my Irish informants' reactions to the knowledge that I lived alone throughout my fieldwork. Almost every informant asked, "Aren't you terribly lonely?" My response of "well, no, I'm well used to it and indeed I like it" was usually met by a shake of the head, deep sympathy, and (from what I could tell) a sincere invitation to "call over" without advance notice should I feel lonely. On the occasions upon which I took up the invitation, and my informants were home, I was welcomed into whatever conversations were taking place and whatever refreshments were available. Callers, particularly pitiable lonely ones such as myself, in my experience, were ushered in heartily and sincerely with enthusiasm, grace, sociability, and no little joking.

7. "Rathkelly" is a composite neighborhood, a pseudonym I use for actual Dublin neighborhoods to protect confidentiality.

8. The rate of home ownership in Ireland is phenomenal, given the high rate of unemployment and comparatively low average wage. Close to 80% of Irish people own, or are buying, their residence (Curry 1993:54), even those on the dole or in low-paying jobs.

9. It is not unusual to receive an energy bill of over £200 (approximately $360) for two months in the winter months. Overall, 2.7% of the annual Gross Domestic Product was estimated to be spent on fuel (World Bank 1995:164).

10. Informants told me that nixers are acceptable to most inhabitants of Rathkelly; in fact, several of them painted or wallpapered houses, or sold crafts, strictly for cash. Getting ahead of the tax man is fine; however, relying entirely on illegal activities is not. Nixers are illegal because they involve earning wages when one is on the dole or should otherwise be reporting the income.

11. Parents are still somewhat reluctant to participate and are often actively discouraged from participating in secondary school administration. Even in primary schools, Catholic religious orders hold most of the power in both daily and long-term planning of curricula, funding, and the physical plant. Even those informants involved in school boards said that they did not feel that they had any influence at all over the curricula or administration of their children's schools. See Inglis (1987) for a more complete discussion.

12. The following observations regarding bus travel in Dublin were discussed with a group of 24 Irish university students in October 1994, and they agreed with my remarks.

13. A conductor on a "two-man" Dublin bus collects fares, leaving the driver responsible only for driving. I have only seen conductors on busy routes, and only during the day. Conductors watch embarking passengers seemingly casually yet are able to identify those passengers who have paid their fare and those who have not.

CHAPTER 5

Public and Private in Dublin: An Overview

As argued in Chapter 1, it is social interaction based on statuses and role relationships (Swartz 1991:6–17) that determines the "public" and "private" nature of social life. "Public" and "private" in the Republic of Ireland, and indeed universally, are aspects of social relationships identifiable through examination of the nature of social relationships (see Wikan 1990:58–62 regarding Bali). The statuses applied in interaction influence what is discussed, how it is discussed, and whether participants characterize and experience a discussion as more or less private or public. The physical space occupied by the participants is less important than the nature of the role relationship between the participants. The relationship between two or more persons[1] shapes the understanding of that relationship as more or less public or private.

To identify an interaction as containing more or fewer private and public aspects, we need some information regarding the cultural understandings at work. We need to know what statuses, and therefore which role relationships, are being used by the participants. We need to know the specific cultural understandings that guide statuses and role relationships. Finally, we need to know how members of the society in question understand whether an interaction is more or less public or private. I provided broad etic definitions for understanding the blending of public and private interaction in Chapter 1, noting that more private interactions will always be composed of generalized reciprocity and general expectations; more public interactions will consist of more limited and specific reciprocity and expectations. In addition, I argue that public and private dimensions blend in ways in which social scientists dealing with the subject have not anticipated. Generalized reciprocity and general expectations, however, are composed of specific behaviors, emotions, and thoughts that vary cross-culturally. There are specific Irish understandings regarding general expectations and intimate emotional behaviors. In this chapter I discuss some of those specific Irish social interactions that demonstrate the complex blending of public and private elements of understandings in social life.

ASPECTS OF PUBLICNESS AND PRIVATENESS IN DUBLIN

Here, I analyze four kinds of social interaction in normal Irish interaction. These relate to a refinement of the analytic distinction of what are putatively Western definitions (but see Strathern 1984) of "public" and "private" in anthropology. The social interactions described below can be broken down into interpenetrating categories. Almost entirely public cultural understandings guide one set; another kind is guided by more public understandings than private ones. A third kind is shaped by more private understandings than public ones, and a final type shows almost entirely private understandings.[2] Through the identification of public and private elements in interaction, we can classify statuses and associated role relationships as more or less public or private. There is a large intermediate range of statuses, role relationships, and interactions in which a blend of public and private elements is more flexible. In this large range, people use understandings about public and private elements in different proportions, based on their conscious, preconscious, and unconscious judgments of what elements are appropriate for the role relationship and for the situation. Different dimensions of public and private are displayed depending on the interaction. The examples below illustrate my general analytic principles for looking at interaction, while in later chapters I concentrate on family role relationships.

The typology of social interaction assumes that an analysis of role relationships will identify public and private elements of an interaction. While role relationships are composed of statuses, it is the actual interaction of the occupants of statuses, guided by the cultural expectations associated with role relationships, that is salient to the more or less public nature of the interaction. It is not statuses that are "public" or "private." So, for example, a mother may discuss her son's progress in school with the son's teacher. The role relationship here is "mother–teacher." One status, "mother," conventionally is seen as belonging in the private, familial, domestic sphere. But the other, "teacher," is a paid position and therefore arguably a public one, if we believe that employment statuses are public. Yet the interaction does not fit into a neat dichotomy. It is neither solely public nor solely private but instead lies instead between the two, containing aspects of cultural understandings about public and private social arenas.

The Irish experience of the private, discussed more fully in later chapters, is in contestation currently as partners in intimate relationships in Ireland rapidly adjust to tremendous social and cultural change. It is the "Dublin 4 lot"—that is, the urban upwardly mobile middle and upper-middle classes[3]—who aspire to an intimate relationship that involves, among other things, Irish conceptions of American psychotherapeutic values regarding romantic and marital relationships such as open communication, egalitarianism, and honest expression of feelings.[4] The new kind of marriage requires that there be little that is truly private, which remains with the individual, revealed to no one (or so the idealized conception goes). It does not fit well with Irish understandings regarding emotional revelation. See Chapter 8 for a discussion of emotional expression.

THE FULLY PUBLIC

The Irish are reticent about revealing feelings in general, as will be shown. This is particularly true in interactions with almost entirely public elements of understandings. The fully public encompasses social situations in which people interact who know each other casually, little, or not at all. Little information of a "private" nature is revealed. The fully public can be anywhere. It can be the Point, a large theater in which rock concerts are staged in Dublin; it could be the bank or supermarket queue; it could be the first-year undergraduate anthropology classroom; it could be the pub, either a "local" or one in the more anonymous City Centre; it can be a person's sitting room, depending on the constituents. It is not dependent on physical space. Social situation and context determine its fully public nature; Unni Wikan (1990) has made analogous analyses of Balinese understandings of public and private. Dubliners do not choose such fully public situations for discussion of intimate issues, as understood by the Irish, regardless of whom they are with.

Instead, there is what I call an "anonymous friendliness" reflected in Irish sociability. Anonymous friendliness obtains in the fully public, and it is marked by the inevitable chat between strangers about the weather, the groceries being purchased, the "brilliant" seats in the

Point or other large rock venues, the idiocy of Irish politicians—usually raised in the pub when the news comes onto the telly—or the subject matter of the lecture in the classroom. On airline flights between London and Dublin, there seem to be three patterns of interaction in this "fully public" social arena: 1) there is no chat whatsoever. This is unusual and usually involves the Dublin 4 lot, "Brits," or "foreigners" of one ilk or another; 2) an initial chat that establishes where the seat partners are from and whom they probably know in common[5]; 3) a long and involved chat dealing with the dreadful winter and hopes—thought to be probably dashed, given the dour summer previously—for a good summer this year. The Irish cultural understanding regarding proper sociability means that a fully public conversation can take place between two strangers. This is anonymous friendliness.

I witnessed anonymous friendliness constantly during my fieldwork. I seemed to blend in rather well in Ireland, usually passing for Irish. Consequently, my experiences in the fully public in Ireland match, to some extent, I was told by informants, those of "real" Irish people and are useful data for this analysis. One incident in particular stands out. On one Saturday morning early in my fieldwork, I was shopping for groceries at a huge supermarket in Lucan (a far western suburb of County Dublin) called Superquinn. I had invited some friends over to dinner for the following evening, and I had included in my purchases adequate quantities of beer and wine, as well as the food for the dinner besides my more mundane household purchases. At the check-out, the clerk and I made brief eye contact as she completed the transaction ahead of me. For the first minute or two of my transaction, the clerk scanned my groceries without comment. Soon, however, she came to one of the wines I had selected. "Ah," she said, "so it's a romantic evening you're in fer." I smiled and shook my head "no." She held my eye for a moment and winked. A brief silence ensued, and then she clutched the beer. "That's for himself, then, is it," she said with a flat finality. Another wink. A few more items were scanned without comment. However, another bottle of wine appeared and the checker clutched it, scanning it and then waving it at me. "Ah," she said, with yet another wink, "you'll be well oiled tonight. Himself with his lager, you with your wine. It'll be a grand evening altogether." The understanding the clerk was using was that, to get true romance, a good Irish woman has to "oil" the evening with drink. "Sure," she implied, "the lads have to be encouraged like" (with alcohol) if they're going to be any kind of partners at all. This is an understanding Irish women share, even those who do not know each other at all.

This instance illustrates the fully public for Ireland. Two people who know each other not at all engage in an interaction that calls upon Irish cultural understandings about what is properly spoken about in the fully public and what is appropriate anonymous friendliness. In the fully public, Irish people expect that they may make general, and usually joking, comments about what objective materials (e.g., wine and beer) may mean without their conversational partner taking offense at the raising of "private" issues, such as the real reason for purchasing wine and beer.

Public elements shaped this interaction. Expectations were specific: the clerk expected a bit of chat, the content of which was influenced by our mutual status as women. The long line of customers prevented a more in-depth conversation, and such a conversation was not expected. Because of this, a second public element can be seen. Not only was the interaction based on specific expectations, but it was time-limited. The clerk did not expect that we would meet later to discuss our lives. Reciprocity, too, was specific. In exchange for the goods I had selected, the clerk collected cash from me. Specific and concrete expectations shaped this fully public interaction.

Queues further illustrate the fully public. During fieldwork, I had ample opportunity to participate in the details of Irish everyday life as I stood in bank, supermarket, and shop queues (people standing in line). In these queues, Irish people expect to engage in "chat" with their fellow queue partners. Although there are no explicit sanctions against not chatting, Irish people expect to, and are expected to, either initiate or respond to comments about the length of the queue, what is being bought, or, most often, the weather. If the sun is shining, it is commonly accepted that the weather is "gorgeous," "grand," or "beautiful." What is important is that one engages in the chat.

The examples of the Superquinn and the queues show the elements that help us see public kinds of interactions, as well as acceptable topics of conversations between strangers. The weather or one's purchases are typical discussions held between people in the fully public. This kind of interaction, marked by anonymous friendliness, calls into play stereotypical statuses that are subtly judged through assessment of physical appearance and dress. The "chat" is the overriding concern; sociability and identification of a person's status are paramount. Individuality is crucial here, while specific statuses, though important in cognitive identification, seem relatively irrelevant to the social interaction. Instead, sociability, anonymous friendliness, is paramount. The *identification* of the status of one's chat partner, and not the specific status held, is crucial to continue chat, to employ anonymous friendliness. Through the queue chat, an Irish person confirms herself as a properly friendly person, an important Irish cultural understanding. At the same time, she reveals little of importance. She can never be sure if the queue partner is a relation of her husband's brother-in-law's cousin's dentist down the country, so she says little that may come back to her.[6] One must be careful then to be properly social in the fully public but to reveal little.

BLENDS OF PUBLIC AND PRIVATE ELEMENTS

This conversational protectiveness obtains in interactions that blend public and private elements as well, though to a lesser extent. This blend can be seen in a party, a group dinner, or, most often, the typical Irish pub session in which a fairly large group of friends and acquaintances meet. One of the many pub sessions[7] in which I participated demonstrates the blending of public and private elements. In these instances, there are more public than private aspects evident.

This session (*seisean*), in spring 1994, drew together people who were at varying levels of intimacy, making it a good example of the mixture of public and private. At its height in the early evening on a Friday night, this session included at least ten people. Some had not met before, though most people had at least met once before, and several were good friends with at least one other person in the group. I had met all but one of the people at least once before. The group was primarily single or separated persons; there were two married women (without their husbands).

People in this group rarely called upon marital or parental statuses and role relationships in conversation. Instead, people broke into smaller groups and had conversations, marked physically by turning away from the larger group and facing one's conversational partner. There was no general group discussion, though people frequently broke off from their smaller groups to comment on a loudly proclaimed "truth" or to respond to requests for rounds.[8] Because discussions were often broken into, and were expected to be broken into, by other group members, little of a personal or intimate nature could be discussed.

For a short time, I spoke with a young woman whom I had met once before. Theresa[9] is in her mid-20s and single. Blond and slightly overweight, she works with a woman who is involved with the brother-in-law of an informant. I asked Theresa how things were going: "how's the craic?"[10] She talked primarily about getting drunk most nights and going to nightclubs. "It's great, really," she said. "I live out near Walkinstown [a western area of Dublin that is suburban in atmosphere] with my sisters; my parents are a ten-minute walk away. It's a nice security, knowing they're there." "Ah, sure," I said, "but they're not down your necks." Theresa nodded. "Yeh," she said, "but it's nice to know you can go down for the tea [the evening meal] and you'll be welcome. You don't have to talk about anything, Mammy and Daddy will do all of it." Still, Theresa said, she's looking around for her own flat closer in. "I like the nightclubs," she told me. We talked about the nightclub scene for a while, and we agreed that "it's good craic." You never meet anyone interesting, but if you're with a group of people it's grand. We were interrupted at that point by a question from one of our number: "you right?" he asked, meaning, do we want another pint? We both assented, and Theresa excused herself to go to the ladies' room. While she was gone, the group rearranged itself so that someone else was sitting next to me when she returned.

In this semipublic setting, dyads and triads are constantly shifting. It is "not on" (unacceptable, not the thing to do) to get involved in a deep discussion with one or two other people. The conversation must be, or appear to be, interruptable. To do otherwise implies that a person is being greedy, by demanding too much attention from one person.

Statuses, too, shift. In my conversation with Theresa, we invoked our mutual status as "single woman." Theresa also called upon her status as "sister" and "flatmate" (which in this case contained some similar elements, since Theresa lived in a flat with her sister). Theresa further discussed her work as a bookkeeper, so that the status "professional" was used; it seemed to be assumed that I, as an educated person, held a similar status.[11] There were several statuses being used as Theresa blended elements of public and private understandings in our inter-action. Although it could be argued that "friend" was a salient status, this does not appear to be the case. In this instance, people were friendly with each other, but they were not all "friends" with each other and did not intend to strike up new friendships.

In other sessions, the group of friends was smaller. One couple whom I came to know well often invited the same five or six people for a few pints. Although they, like all of my informants, occasionally hosted din-ners, usually centered on watching sporting events on television, the pub session was the most common way to socialize. This group con-sisted of two married or cohabiting couples and several single or sep-arated people, all of whom worked with at least one other person in the group. In other words, everyone in the group had a connection with someone in the group. Oftentimes these ties were long-standing. Ad-ditionally, each session was almost always discussed in depth the next day among the participants.

The male partner[12] of the couple organizing the sessions, Diarmuid, had a tendency to become boisterous and raucous after the fourth pint or so. Rosemary, his partner, became more quiet as Diarmuid grew louder. Rosemary worked for Paul, who goaded Diarmuid into drinking more and into stating opinions vociferously. There was a general pat-tern to each session. Diarmuid usually began pontificating on general issues of the biological differences between men and women. After he had established—with a sly twinkle in his eye—that men were superior to women biologically and that women are the natural caretakers of children, he crescendoed to his party piece, his strong disapproval of divorce and separation despite his own five year separation. Paul generally nodded vigorously in agreement throughout, glancing at the self-admitted "feminists" in the group (university-educated or professional women). Towards the end of evenings, Diarmuid became morose and argumentative, saying that he regretted leaving his wife and six children in Waterford but that there was no alternative. No one argued with him but instead would begin to look uncomfortable, shifting in chairs and glancing at one another. Paul, himself separated, offered the same consolation every time: "Well, but yeh look after your children every weekend, don't yeh?" "But it's all wrong," Diarmuid invariably replied. "Rosemary, you're the greatest, don't get me wrong. But marriages should be forever." Despite Diarmuid's apparently genuine concern for his children, he would not be comforted after his brief outburst. His earlier arguments—that women should be the nurturers of children—did not apply to his own situation.

The next day, participants discussed the previous evening's events. After one session that was particularly long, Mae, who had business relationships with Diarmuid, Rosemary, and Paul, analyzed Diarmuid's behavior. "We don't take him too seriously when he's had his few pints. That's just how he is. The drink will do it to yeh," she commented. Although Mae never revealed anything very personal in the group, despite drinking herself, she did not find Diarmuid's behavior remarkable or shameful. She would never castigate Diarmuid or remind him of what he had said, she said: "It's the drink. He doesn't mean it." Mairead, Mae's business partner, offered a similar analysis: "Diarmuid gets a jar down him and he can't control himself. If he gets too silly next time, I might mention the last time. But he doesn't mean it, and it's best forgotten." In the next session, indeed, Diarmuid's overly emotional behavior was not mentioned.

In these pub sessions, this group of Dubliners notices what they consider inappropriate behavior, but they do not confront the issue. They blame "the drink" for Diarmuid's revelation of emotions. At the same time, because Diarmuid has discussed his feelings about marriage and divorce so often, the material has become, in some ways, more public. Diarmuid violates ideal expectations for what friends may and may not talk about, through revealing his emotions, but his friends do not take his talk seriously. Even though most of these relationships began as work-related and contained many elements of public understandings, the role relationship "friend–friend" has changed so that elements of private understandings guide behavior in this group. Poor behavior, like Diarmuid's, is ignored, and the group uses its knowledge of what "the drink" can do to place Diarmuid's behavior within acceptable limits. This shows that private and public understandings blend in specific and complex ways.

Another arena in which elements of public and private understandings mix in interesting ways are in the small shops that many people in Rathkelly use. There are no large supermarkets in the area like the Superquinn described above; the closest large grocery is in the City Centre at St. Stephen's Green shopping center. Because most families remain in the same neighborhood over a number of years, and often in the same house, people develop role relationships with shopowners, shopkeepers, and clerks that last for many years. One family, the Kenneys, with whom I worked, had lived in their house for fourteen years and had been walking to the same market for their groceries over that period. Usually the wife, Grainne, did the marketing every day, although she would send one of her six children for minor items now and then. She knew Brian, the news agent, not only from her shopping but also because they attended the same church and because their children were classmates at school. Grainne knew Tom, the butcher, and again they were fellow worshipers. She further had known Séan, the greengrocer, since she had moved into the neighborhood. When Grainne came into each shop, the shopkeeper always made a comment about the weather to her unless he was otherwise occupied with another customer. They would discuss the weather at length; often other customers joined in. The shopkeeper would then inquire after Grainne's health: "How're yeh keeping, Grainne?" Her response was always positive, and she would say, "I'm well now, how're yeh?" Next the shopkeeper asked about her husband and the children; Grainne invariably responded, "Ah, they're grand. How're your lot?" After a brief response from the shopkeeper, usually "Ah, they're grand," she would then commence her shopping. After paying for her purchases, perhaps discussing the menu for tea (supper), the shopkeeper usually would say goodbye with "safe home now."

This role relationship, "shopkeeper–customer," is an instance of the complex mixture of public and private understandings in Irish social life. The relationships between Grainne and the various shopkeepers have existed for a long time; the shopkeepers and Grainne know details of each other's life. The shopkeepers ask sociable questions about the Kenneys, as she does about their family. These questions are guided by understandings that are partly private in nature and partly public. The shopkeepers have general information about Grainne's family that people outside her network would not have; the shopkeepers possess some private information. At the same time, the shopkeepers and Grainne understand that the shop is not the place to discuss the family in detail. There are public elements in the understandings guiding this role relationship: the interaction is time-limited and interruptable, and the participants understand that they each have specific and concrete goals in addition to sociability. The shopkeepers ultimately want to receive cash or welfare vouchers in exchange for the items Grainne wants to purchase. The role relationship "shopkeeper–customer" is, therefore, guided by both public and private elements—perhaps by more public understandings than private ones.

The previous interactions contain more public elements than private ones. There are some types of interactions in Dublin that have more private elements than public ones. In these kinds of interactions, Dubliners call upon more solidified or general statuses.[13] A male–female dyad will engage in more "personal" interaction based in part on expectations of the conversational partner's emotional or intellectual understandings centered in understandings concerning "natural" male and female behaviors. Members of dyads may discuss particular personalities, and their reactions to them, at work. They talk generally about their spouses, their children, or their friends. In short, in these kinds of interactions, Dubliners discuss what they consider more "personal" issues, using understandings about role relationships shaped by private elements more than public ones.

These sorts of interactions are usually limited either to mixed-gender or to woman–woman discussions. Several of my male informants told me that they do not discuss anything of substance with their male friends and instead focus their conversation on sports, politics, cars, or "the craic." Dublin men said that they speak openly only with women friends, when they and their friends are meeting alone.[14] One informant talked very openly about his relationship with his ex-wife and his subsequent "lady friends" when no other friends were with us. He said that he talked about such things with his two or three good female friends as well, although, he added, he is not as open with his Irish women friends as he was with me.[15] He went on to say that he does not and never would discuss things such as his frustrations with his ex-wife or current girlfriend, however, either with a male friend or in a wider group. He would not bring up such subjects in a group larger than a dyad, and that dyad must be male–female.

Similarly, several women disclosed to me, over time, details of their lives when we met with no one else present. They all told me that "nobody else" knows the things they told me in the way they have told me about them. In almost all cases, we have discussed life histories alone, with no one else around, usually when "well oiled" (discussed above). Several statuses were operating at one time—Irish person, American, friend, professional person. A master, (partially) shared status of "woman," which my friends seemed to think transcended nationality, was primary, however, and it facilitated communication.

My friends and I shared understandings about how women communicate with each other. We listen. We do not interrupt. We nod in agreement and in encouragement to continue. We gaze, when not speaking, at the speaker with interest and empathy, but we do not look too long. We do not make judgments. We do not offer criticisms. We pick up on partial sentences and complete them in an attempt to further the speaker's narrative. A particularly Irish response is a sharp intake of breath, with a partially verbalized "yeh," at specifically important or poignant parts of the speaker's narrative. Such a response indicates "yes, I'm listening, yes, you're right, oh, how awful, oh, how brilliant, that's grand" (whatever the appropriate response is to what is being said). The intake of breath is a marker of attention on the part of the listener. It is used only in dyadic or, more rarely, in triadic conversation and interactions.

These conversational markers are identifiers that define statuses called into play in social interaction. In interactions with a preponderance of private elements in Ireland among women or in mixed-gender dyads, one is expected to listen and to appear to be listening. One rarely will offer judgments about the person speaking. Sympathy, in these interactions, is offered briefly with a curt nod of the head, a small grimace, or a quick statement of the problem being described. The status "friend" is being used. For example, in the instance discussed above in which one of my friends told me her life story, although she discussed her activities as a mother, as a daughter, and as a worker, she did not call upon the expectations and understandings relating to "mother," "daughter," or "employee" when talking with me. Instead, we were employing the status of "friend," and the role relationship "friend–friend." "Friend" is the primary status, showing that the more private elements in relationships are a clear mixture of private and public aspects.[16]

THE PRIVATE

Marital and familial statuses such as "mother," "daughter," "father," "husband," "wife," and "son" sharpen into the private by the use of elements of private understandings in specific role relationships. For example, "mother–son" contains more private aspects than does "mother–teacher." I discuss these statuses, and a few of the many role relationships associated with them, in subsequent chapters. It is important to note, however, that "private" relationships are undergoing some change currently. Both "traditional" and "modern" kinds of "private" understandings obtain in Irish society today. What mothers, wives, fathers, and husbands are expected to, and expect to, do, think, and feel is changing rapidly.

One 45-year-old woman told me that she believed that expectations relating to her status as "mother" had been altered in Irish society only within the last five to seven years, though there was talk of change "by the women's libbers" before that. She believes that her teenaged daughter will expect entirely different behaviors of both herself and her eventual partner in the space of just a few years.

Men, too, are faced with changes in expectations and understandings about what they are meant to do. "I just don't know what to do anymore," one working-class man in his late thirties told me. "I thought I was going to be the breadwinner, take care of my family, work at my job and come home to tea on the table. That's how it should be, but that's not how it's happening." This man entered marriage some ten years ago with clear understandings of what a husband and father is supposed to do. He now is unsure, aware that marriage and parenthood are being altered and separated rather quickly.

For this man, and for many Dubliners, the status "father" and the status "husband" are tied up together despite growing pressure to separate them. Still, for most men, behaviors expected from both statuses are similar: providing well for the family, working, doing maintenance outside the house, leaving the child rearing to the wife. A man is not a proper husband if he is also not a father. It appears that the difference between "father" and "husband" lies primarily in the fact that a "husband" has sex with his "wife." The idealized "American-style" marriage discussed above is thought to be important in Dublin 4 quarters. However, emphasis in Irish cultural understandings continues to be placed on "family" much more so than on "marriage."

In this chapter, I outlined a typology that demonstrates the complex mixture of public and private interaction in Dublin. Rather than assuming that a strict dichotomy guides interaction in various social arenas, I demonstrated that identification of role relationships places an interaction in the fully public, blends of public and private expectations and understandings, and the private. Most interactions are neither solely public nor solely private. Moreover, in Ireland, as in every society, even the most public interactions contain understandings regarding proper sociability. Finally, understandings regarding what is properly revealed, and what is kept to oneself, influence interaction. I turn now to motherhood, ostensibly on a "private" status. As will be seen, however, the everyday life of Irish mothers is more complicated than that.

NOTES

1. Even if a person is not specifically interacting with someone else at a particular time, behavior, thoughts, and emotions remain firmly grounded in

interactional understandings. I assume that almost all behaviors, cognition, and feeling states are guided by cultural understandings, which are entirely social in nature. Thus, even if a person is performing some act that could be construed either locally or universally as entirely private in nature—writing in a diary, masturbating, fantasizing—such acts are shaped by cultural understandings which guide that person's actions. Although certain physiological acts can be seen reasonably as based in irreducible biological necessity—and therefore presocial—this is not actually the case. Defecation and, to a lesser extent, urination, are probably almost universally individual, private acts based on individual biophysical urges; however, whether one defecates or urinates near other people, how one feels about these acts, and how one understands the products—feces and urine—of these acts can be variable.

2. Further, there is a realm of privacy that is marked not by overt social interaction but by what is withheld from discussion with anyone, including, and sometimes especially, a spouse. Such a realm of privacy is contrary to social scientific constructions of the "domestic" or the "private" as the emotional or intimate realm of Western "private" life (see Chapter 1).

3. This group is the "Dublin 4 lot" because most of Dublin's intelligentsia lives on the south side of the city, in middle-class areas, with the postal code of Dublin 4. My informants used the term both defensively and derisively for the most part; one laughingly said, "it's a state of mind, not a postal code."

4. American sociologist Frank Furstenberg summarized surveys of American middle-class couples and found that 50% of wives and 47% of husbands interviewed prefer an egalitarian marriage in which household chores and economic contributions are equal (Furstenberg 1996:40). He concluded that "both men and women enter marriage with higher expectations of interpersonal communication, intimacy, and sexual gratification" as a result of the American middle-class trend toward egalitarian marriage (Furstenberg 1996: 40). It is reasonable to assume that the Irish hear about these American expectations through American talk shows with psychotherapeutic orientations, such as *Oprah* and *Sally Jesse Raphael*, both of which frequently feature psychologists commenting on guests' problems and both of which appear on Irish television regularly.

5. Quite often they are able to place each other almost immediately and are able to provide innocuous gossip for the entire trip. Ireland, as I was reminded frequently, "is a small place, really."

6. This may be related to the long history of oppressive British colonial occupation. It could be that the British presence for 400 years here helped develop what I am calling "anonymous friendliness." Because an Irish person never knew how the person being spoken to might be related to the colonial powers, one might have needed to develop indirect "checking-out" communicational styles, and it could be that they tended to hold back much more than they revealed. A check on the very small literature base analyzing social relations and colonialism in Ireland shows no discussion of the effect of colonialism on Irish behavior and cultural understandings. However, in the context of colonialism, which continues to be important to Irish cultural understandings today, such an indirect communication style makes sense. Irish people seem to

understand what is being asked, and they know how to respond without apparent overwhelming psychological conflict.

7. It should be remembered that a good deal of Dublin—and, in general, Irish male—social life revolves around the pub. This is not, however, an indication of a peculiarly Irish propensity for "the drink" (Clare 1993:6–7). Many times people will meet in the pub and some will have tea, coffee, or soft drinks. At the same time, most Irish people I have met are not adverse to "a quick pint," which usually means three or four pints of Guinness or lager and a good two and half hours at the "local," the neighborhood pub. However, these sessions most often occur after a large evening meal and do not lead necessarily to drunkenness.

8. It is polite to buy drinks, or a "round," for the group. Unless the group is very large, one person takes responsibility for buying each series of drinks. The next time the group goes out, anyone who did not pay for rounds the last time is expected to buy a round this time. Although this generalized reciprocity obtains between friends, a person who does not meet the round-buying obligation will be dropped from future sessions.

9. All names are pseudonyms.

10. "Craic," pronounced "crack," usually means fun, amusement, or entertainment, or a laugh and a chat. "How's the craic?" is often used to ask "what's going on?" or "how are you?" instead of "what's the news?," another common greeting in Dublin.

11. My statuses as "American," "intellectual/academic," and "researcher" did not seem salient to this interaction. However, my status as "single woman" was highly relevant to the discussion of the nightclub scene. My "American" status seemed far less important than my "single" status.

12. "Partner" is understood by Dubliners to mean lover, usually a live-in lover. When "partner" refers to a business partner, a speaker clarifies the relationship by adding modifiers like "business partner" or "workmate."

13. "Solidified" or "general" statuses can also be "master" statuses. That is, a master status ultimately calls upon intimate understandings regarding gender behavior and motivation. These statuses, which can be distilled down to the expectations and understandings surrounding "man" or "woman," may require more intimate social arenas to be elicited. These arenas enable individuals to extrapolate to semipublic and public expectations of "male" and "female."

14. This of course takes place in other societies as well, but it does occur in Ireland and is part of understandings that shape marital and friend role relationships.

15. As will be seen in Chapter 8, Irish people find emotional expression uncomfortable. I encouraged discussions of emotional life, however, which may have helped my informant feel more relaxed when talking about his romantic life. Further, he may have been relying on my "American" and "outsider" statuses, which may have led him to believe such revelations were safe (as, indeed, they were). Finally, this informant clearly wanted very badly to talk in depth about his feelings, and I tried to help him with that expression.

16. Some, though not all, statuses and role relationships guiding behavior in Dublin workplaces are also a mixture of public and private elements. If the

participants have established a close relationship—such as between a boss and a secretary (see Chapter 1)—it will likely involve socializing and discussion of personal material. We saw that in the discussion of the second pub session, above. However, in the case of "boss–secretary," the role relationships of "friend–friend" and "boss–secretary," though intermingling, have different constituents and understandings. When expectations become blended, fundamental alterations in the role relationships take place. For example, if a secretary becomes friendly with her boss, and the relationship begins to contain more private elements, the secretary may expect her boss to alter his behavior toward and expectations of her. The secretary may expect, for example, the boss to be sympathetic when she is late or performing poorly, calling upon understandings that underlie the role relationship of "friend–friend" rather than "boss–secretary." See Chapter 7 for a discussion of such an alteration of a role relationship.

CHAPTER 6

The Mammy Is the Heart of the Family

Although the Irish usually associate the "mammy" with the domestic arena, Irish mothers interact in a variety of social arenas, using cultural understandings regarding public and private aspects of their behavior. "Mother" is not a unitary status that gives rise to role relationships solely in family life. Rather, different aspects of motherhood in Ireland are elicited depending upon the role relationship and social situation. Mothers act beyond what has been conventionally seen as the private sphere.

In this chapter, I first discuss the ideal general and specific expectations that the Irish hold about the status "mother." This discussion shows that the Irish, and particularly the Catholic Church, associate mothers with the domestic arena almost exclusively. I also present several examples of Irish mothers. The accompanying analyses argue that, in everyday life, Irish mothers employ different aspects of private and public behaviors in the various arenas of their lives. Irish mothers are concerned with behaviors beyond the domestic.

IDEAL EXPECTATIONS REGARDING IRISH MOTHERS

Ideal expectations regarding Irish mothers can be seen as being influenced by several sources. The Catholic Church has been one of the strongest influences. Although it may be argued that the Church's influence in 1990s Ireland is diminishing, the legacy of Church authority over the cultural understandings surrounding motherhood remains (Inglis 1987). The Church took an active interest in shaping Irish motherhood in the nineteenth century as part of a general wish to prove to the British its ability to "civilize" Irish peasants (Inglis 1987:200–205). The Catholic Church continues to attempt to shape Irish motherhood.

Those women who do not enter religious life have one appropriate option in the Church's view: motherhood is the only other choice available for women. Although motherhood is a less blessed occupation than religious life, the Church argues that it can provide salvation through submission to one's husband and the Church (Beale 1986:50; Urbine and Seifert 1993:84). Work outside the home, on the other hand, is fundamentally degrading to women, in the Church's view.[1] Pope John Paul II, in his visit to the Republic in 1979, told Irish women that work outside the home was demeaning to their very womanhood: "May Irish mothers, young women and girls not listen to those who tell them that working at a secular job, succeeding in a secular profession, is more important than the vocation of giving life and caring for this life as a mother" (cited in Beale 1986:50). Moreover, John Paul II continues to argue against women working outside the home: "Furthermore, the mentality which honors women more for their work outside the homes than for their work within the family must be overcome" (John Paul II 1982:21). The Church believes that female nature is suited to the kind of service only realized through motherhood. In a guide to interpreting John Paul II's exhortations, William Urbine and William Seifert note that John Paul II has stated that "through virginity and motherhood, women fulfill their humanity" and that "woman was called into creation as man's helper" (Urbine and Seifert 1993:83–84). The Church remains firmly committed to the idea that a woman is fulfilled only through celibacy and/or mothering.

Some informants echoed this belief. One working-class man in his late thirties told me that women who think they want careers, particularly as teachers, do not want any such thing at all: "It's a substitute like for the maternal instinct, it's the taking care of people not the career that's important." This same man, a separated, noncustodial father of two, said another time that "it's unnatural for women to be interested in life outside of the home—it's the bonding yeh see, it's natural for a woman to be the childrearer. She wouldn't want really to be away from the babas." In this view, shared by most, though not all, Irish men and women with whom I worked, men, being "naturally" aggressive, are suited to the "outside" world of work, while women are biologically designed to be nurturing. Women cannot perform adequately outside the home because of "nature."

The Church agrees. Women are biologically built to serve and help men, in the Church's view. Pope John XXIII continues to be cited by the Irish Catholic Church as having offered the definitive statement on the natural role for women: "Woman as a person enjoys a dignity equal with men, but she was given different tasks by God and by Nature, which perfect and complete the work entrusted to men" (cited in McCafferty 1987:21). This idea remains in the most recent Catholic Catechism as well (*Catechism of the Catholic Church* 1994:§371–372). Those tasks are motherhood, and solely motherhood, should a vocation to religious life not be received. Women are meant to assist men in worldly tasks, not to initiate their own, independent work (Urbine and Seifert 1993:84).

A mother, as the Church defines her, is to be the heart of the family, offering support and love to her husband, children, and parents. Beale, basing her remarks on interviews with 27 Irish women, says that, much like the Virgin Mary, after whom Catholic mothers should model themselves: "mother is the spiritual and emotional foundation for the family, the source of love and affection and of moral values. It is to her that members of the family can turn when in trouble or distress. . . . It is an ideal which is clearly modeled on the image of Mary as mother of Jesus . . . [who had] an essentially submissive motherhood" (Beale 1986:50–51). "Mother," then, as understood by the Catholic Church Hierarchy and by many Irish people, is, like the Virgin Mary (*Catechism of the Catholic Church* 1994:§494), self-sacrificing, suppressing her needs, instructing her children, helping and obeying her husband, and is the emotional wellspring for the family, never demanding anything on her own account.

The Irish Catholic Church has been able to codify its understanding of "woman" as "mother." As discussed in Chapter 2, the Irish Constitution, enacted in 1937, was jointly written by the Irish government and the Hierarchy. The family is seen to be the basic, irreducible unit of Irish society, and Irish law protects that unit at almost all costs (Dillon 1993:23). In addition, the articles of the Irish constitution dealing with the family use "woman" and "mother" interchangeably. Article 41 of the Constitution, entitled "The Family," shows this. Prior to the 1995 referendum on divorce, Article 41 in its entirety read as follows:

1. 1. The State recognises the Family as the natural primary and fundamental unit group of Society, and as a moral institu-

tion possessing inalienable and imprescriptible rights, antecedent and superior to all positive law.

2. The State, therefore, guarantees to protect the Family in its constitution and authority, as the necessary basis of social order and as indispensable to the welfare of the Nation and the State.

2. 1. In particular, the State recognises that by her life within the home, *woman* gives to the State a support without which the common good cannot be achieved.

2. The State shall, therefore, endeavour to ensure that *mothers* shall not be obliged by economic necessity to engage in labour to the neglect of their duties in the home.

3. 1. The State pledges itself to guard with special care the institution of Marriage, on which the Family is founded, and to protect it against attack.

2. No law shall be enacted providing for the grant of a dissolution of marriage.[2]

3. No person whose marriage has been dissolved under the civil law of any other State but is a subsisting valid marriage under the law for the time being in force within the jurisdiction of the Government and Parliament established by this Constitution shall be capable of contracting a valid marriage within that jurisdiction during the lifetime of the other party to the marriage so dissolved. (Article 41, Constitution of Ireland 1990:138; italics added)

The Church, through the State, clearly asserts that women are naturally created for one purpose should the religious life evade them: women should be mothers, and only mothers.

Ideals surrounding the Irish mammy spring up even outside Church rhetoric. Informants report that the ideal mammy is a self-sacrificing, "loving," strong, emotionally inexpressive woman. She will go without proper clothing or footwear, and for that matter without a meal, so that her children and, secondarily, her husband, may be warm and fed. It is through her actions rather than her words that an Irish mammy is identified. She is responsible for all household tasks—cooking, cleaning, gardening, barn work (if rural), minding the fire, sewing, mending, knitting, *ad infinitum*. She typically has a soft spot for her sons and is harsher with her daughters. With regard to her daughters, the idealized Irish mammy sounds very much like the "training" mother outlined by Beatrice Whiting and Carolyn Edwards in their update of the Six Cultures study (1988:93–128).[3] She seems much more a "sociable"

(Whiting and Edwards 1988) if not indulgent mother toward her sons. Both styles would be overlain with a "controlling" maternal style. Daughters, in the idealized view, are taught early on to do chores around the house while sons would not be responsible for any adult tasks, either those understood as "female" or "male" until they are at least twelve years old. The idealized Irish mammy rules the roost; her husband does not participate in the household very much.

This idealized view is confirmed in Mary Loughane's work (1983). In short-term fieldwork interviews[4] with a variety of mothers, Loughane reports that Irish women repeatedly said that the mother is the heart of the home. One of Loughane's informants said that "the woman is the focal point of the home, the ultimate authority after God . . ." (Loughane 1983:101). Another informant reported that she should be "the heart and soul of her family since if the woman is 'no good' then the home is a disaster" (Loughane 1983:107). Loughane's informants indicate that the mother is meant to be the source of love and comfort,[5] the adult hand guiding the course of the entire family.[6]

Mothers, then, are idealized for the most part as strong, stoic, self-sacrificing, loving, and in charge, all as part of the natural process of maternal instinct and femininity. Direct identifications with the Virgin Mary are not drawn quite so clearly in the secular cultural view as in the Church view of motherhood. Nonetheless, the Irish mother is surrounded by clear cultural understandings that suggest ideal behaviors and motivations for the status "mother." It should be noted, however, that the Irish are beginning to redraw the ideal general and specific expectations of motherhood. Some younger mothers, particularly those in middle-class Dublin areas, are adopting idealized norms of sociability and friendship rather than authority and strong self-sacrifice with their young children.

I turn now to several examples of motherhood in different generations. Behavior and interactions in work, shopping, and home arenas show that this status, like all statuses used in multiplex relationships, has many components. The status "mother" in Dublin is composed of a blend of public and private elements in most role relationships.

JEANNE O'BRIEN

Jeanne is a 25-year-old widow with an eight-year-old daughter and a two-year-old son. Jeanne is relatively tall for an Irishwoman—approximately 5'8"—of normal weight, with curly long jet-black hair and direct, brilliant blue eyes. She is engaged to be married to a builder, Martín, whom she met through mutual friends. Although she is from "down the country" (from a rural area) and has lived abroad for a number of years, Jeanne has been living in Dublin for the past four years.

Jeanne works on a *Foras Áiseanna Saothair* (FÁS) scheme, a government program in which welfare recipients are employed and "retrained" in different areas. Jeanne works as a teacher's aide in a local school. She lives some distance from the school, however, and does not socialize with her co-workers, although her daughter attends the school. A warm and funny woman, Jeanne has strong opinions about women's issues and rarely calls upon her status as "mother" to support her views. She leans toward a sociable maternal style with her children.

Jeanne invited me to go grocery shopping with her fairly often. During a typical shopping trip, Jeanne rushed through the shop. She usually collects her daughter from school when she is done working. Jeanne helped Judy button her coat, put on her mittens, and adjust her backpack so that it was comfortable. Jeanne slowed her steps so that Judy would not lag behind. Jeanne asked Judy about her day at school, and Judy launched into a convoluted story about a number of schoolmates' antics and the sisters' responses to them (recall that almost all elementary and secondary schools are run by Catholic clergy). Jeanne listened with interest and patience, apparently knowledgeable about the many protagonists. Jeanne also reminded Judy of the various upcoming activities that they had planned, speaking in a friendly and relaxed way.

Upon reaching the shop, Jeanne smiled a hello at one of the clerks but did not take time to chat. Unlike Mrs. Kenney in Chapter 5, Jeanne did not know the shopkeeper and clerks; she did not shop at this larger market very often, but it was on the way home this day. Moving quickly through the grocery, Jeanne collected bread and milk. Judy managed to keep pace, staying out of the way of the older ladies moving more slowly. One older lady smiled at Jeanne, apparently in approval of her daughter's efforts to be well-mannered. At the butcher's counter, Jeanne asked Judy what she wanted for dinner. "We've beefburgers; d'yeh want a beefburger?" she said kindly. "No" was Judy's definite response. "Oh, okay, no beefburger. That'll be for me and Martín. How about lamb chops? I have a couple of lamb chops left. Do you want lamb chops?" Judy nodded her head vigorously, smiling in delight. "Oh, okay, lamb chops it is for you, pet, and Martín and me will have beefburgers. No problem." Jeanne explained that she consults with Judy, which most Dublin mothers wouldn't do. "I always ask her what she wants. There's no point in making her something for tea that she won't eat or doesn't want, and if I can give her the choice I will."

Jeanne, a younger mother, alters both ideal and everyday expectations for the status "mother." Rather than acting as, and believing herself to be, the sole authority in the home, Jeanne asks her daughter about food preferences, accepting Judy's choices with good cheer and equanimity. Few Dublin mothers would take such a consultative posture with their children. Jeanne remarked that "I know I'm in charge. The children are my responsibility; I'm not theirs. But like Judy will notice now when I'm not feeling well or if I seem out of sorts like, and she'll try to make it better . . . And I make sure that I don't talk down to her, that I don't patronize her." Jeanne responds to Judy's concerns honestly but appropriately, she thinks.

Jeanne has abstract as well as prosaic reasons for consulting with her daughter. She explains the supermarket experience partly in political terms:

> So this afternoon like, I asked her what she wanted for dinner. I don't get bothered about little things like that. It doesn't matter to me what she eats for dinner. I want to be training her for choice, and today she can make the choice. It's not that important, and it's teaching her to become comfortable with the choices she makes. That'll serve her well later on in life when bigger choices come up.

Jeanne has strong views about reproductive choice, including abortion: she believes that women should be free to choose. She passionately assails the Catholic Church and what she sees as a patriarchal, traditionally peasant society that allows men to be sexual but not women: "Women aren't supposed to be sexual here. We can't be sexual. We don't discuss it, we don't talk about it with each other or anywhere, really. God help us if we say 'God, I had a great orgasm last night.' We're not supposed to talk about what we want; we're only supposed to have babies." Jeanne is educating her daughter to talk about, be supported in, and act upon what she wants.

Jeanne, like so many Irish informants, says that she does not discuss these views, or indeed any part of her "personal life" in any depth with coworkers. She says that her coworkers know that she has children and that she is getting married, but "Like I wouldn't tell anyone at work about any of this I've told you. I wouldn't be that candid . . . A lot of this I wouldn't want people at work to know. It's not that they're awful or anything, it's just none of their business." Jeanne believes that it is best to keep what she sees as personal away from her co-workers. She deems it prudent to hide her views from her co-workers and from Sister Patricia, her supervisor. Jeanne believes that her beliefs are so different from her colleagues' that she would run the risk of being fired should she express herself: "Well, it's that they love to gossip, and if it ever got back to Sister, well . . ." Jeanne's perception of what is "personal"—her marriage, her child-rearing methods, her engagement— would have conflicted, until very recently, with Church ideas about what behaviors can be appropriately scrutinized by religious authorities. Indeed, her former parish priest felt free to visit her house and correct her child-rearing methods after her husband died. Jeanne tolerated one visit and refused to allow the priest entry the next time he called over. Few Irish mothers would have dared to defy the parish priest in the way Jeanne did. Jeanne no longer attends Mass because she found her priest to be far too intrusive. She has not, however, directly confronted the priest with her concerns; instead, she simply ignores him. Jeanne believes that her family life is separate from her work or spiritual life.

Despite her perception that she keeps her "private life" separate from her work life, Jeanne uses her philosophy and experience as a mother in her work as a teacher's aide. As shown, Jeanne talks with her daughter in a sociable manner. Jeanne contrasts this with Sister Patricia, who works with four-year-olds: "Don't get me wrong: she's a lovely woman. But she expects that children will not express themselves, that four-year-olds can sit quietly and can follow a straight line and walk quietly with one finger on their mouth and the other hand on their heads." Jeanne treats the children differently, in the same way that she interacts with her own children. She attends to the emotional needs of children in her classroom:

> Like there's this one child who is very, very quiet, always sitting in a corner, always looks scared witless. I try to talk to the child, but I get no response. "C'mon into the group," I'll say, but no response. Always looked ready to burst into tears, like a little scared rabbit, wouldn't hug and shrank away from physical contact. But I worked away and worked away and worked away at this child and finally got a smile. I was worried though. [Jeanne relates this child's tragic family history of abuse, death, drug abuse, and instability.]
>
> I approached her very gently. I could see that she'd run if I forced anything. But I could also see that she wanted some adult stable contact. So one day I picked up a soft toy—I think it was an elephant or something. I said to her, "This elephant is very lonely and he needs a cuddle. Do you think you could help?" And she did, she squeezed the bejesus out of it, and—this was the best part—she gave me a smile. I felt like, Jeanne, you've done something here. I was the only one at that school able to reach her.

Jeanne's sociable mothering style has influenced her work. She has taken some private aspects of the status "mother"—her personal belief in the importance of the expression of emotion and in parental sensitivity and respect—and applied them in her work, particularly in the role relationship of "teacher's aide–student." Through observation of a troubled child, Jeanne formulated a "treatment plan" based on her success with her own children.

Jeanne's attitude conflicts with Irish understandings about appropriate childish behavior. Jeanne reports that Sister Patricia did not notice this child:

> She would think that the girl was in fine shape—she was quiet and compliant and didn't cause any trouble. Those are the kinds of children that Sister would consider well-behaved and in no need of anything extra, whereas I would see them as needing some help, because that kind of quietness in a young child is not good. Sister wouldn't like to have the confident ones, the ones who don't really need any help, who can do for themselves but may have a bit of cheek to them. They'd be troublemakers to her, but I'd see them as getting on fine, probably with good families and supportive homes. Otherwise how could they have gotten so confident? But Sister doesn't understand that they're not bold; they're just used to saying what's on their minds, expressing themselves.

Jeanne sees nothing wrong with children who have a "bit of spark about them"; her beliefs run contrary to most Irish ideas about proper behavior of children. Indeed, "bold" children are rare.

Jeanne has adopted a mothering style that is different from most in Dublin. It may be partly due to her youth; it may also be because she has lived a tumultuous life, a good part of it away from Ireland, in Belfast and in London. She uses her maternal style at work, as can be seen in her treatment of the withdrawn girl, without ever revealing very much to her co-workers and supervisors about how she has come to this style. Jeanne's child-rearing methods and philosophies could be related also to her status as "widow." She has more freedom than mothers who have husbands. Regardless, Jeanne's maternal style contrasts with most mothering I observed. Jeanne shows very well how the public world of work is affected by private concerns, experiences, and understandings of motherhood.

MARY EVANS

Mary Evans works in the same school as Jeanne O'Brien. All of Mary's children have attended that school and one remains in the "mixed infants" class, composed of six-and seven-year-old children of both sexes. Mary is some fifteen years older than Jeanne. Married for sixteen years, she and her husband Joe have three children. Mary is lanky, appearing older than her forty-two years, with dyed blond hair that does not match her careworn face. Mary dresses either in a cardigan and skirt or a blazer and skirt, eschewing trousers entirely. She is more comfortable discussing her parents and siblings, her children, her husband, or work issues rather than herself. Like so many Irish people, Mary talks about her life in a businesslike, unemotional way, only slipping in details of her own struggles after several pints. Even those details, however, are delivered in an offhand and humorous way, and she allows no emotional exploration.

Mary is a competent worker, believing that if she is paid a wage, then she should work hard. She also is able to take classes to further her FÁS training while on the job. Mary now works in administration, although she has held other positions in the school. She proudly states that she has a reputation for straight talking: "I'm not scared of nuns, never was really, but some of the other parents listen to me tell Sister Patricia where to get off and their mouths just drop. Don't get me wrong, I have respect for her, I just don't always agree with her." Mary reports that she gets along with the teachers and administration despite her firm ideas. "See," she says, "if Sister Edith [the principal] tells me to do something, and I don't agree, I'll tell her to her face, but Cliona [an assistant] won't do that, not at all. She's jealous of me, I think, that I get on so well with everyone. My contract's been extended but hers won't be because of shite like this." Even though nuns typically do not encourage challenges, Mary has been able to demonstrate her competence and develop good working relationships by stating her position clearly.

Another side of Mary's abilities was shown by a jumble sale that she organized around Christmas. It was held just after school, so several mothers came through the sale with their children. Mary had been talking of little else but the jumble sale for several weeks. She organized the room, obtained donations from parents, convinced other parents to make little arts and crafts, and received permission for this sale from the school administration. She drafted three other workers into minding the tables and arranged for child minding while the sale took place.

On the day of the sale, Mary strode purposively through the room, greeting women by name, chatting about the various items on sale and pointing out the quality of the items, slyly admiring out loud certain more expensive pieces. Sister Edith came in at one point, dressed in a long habit and full wimple. The women in the room barely acknowledged her presence, though their sidelong and slightly fearful glances showed their heightened awareness of the principal. Mary said "hello" to Sister and showed her around the booths. Sister nodded abstractedly and said, vaguely, "You've done a fine job, Mary." "Thank yeh, Sister," Mary replied, "it's turned up well indeed, hasn't it." "Yes, well . . ." Sister said, "Good work. I'll be off now."

Mary consulted with one of her co-workers rather intensely for ten minutes. Although the conversation was inaudible, and Mary and her coworkers kept to a corner of the room, the women at the sale noticed it. No one asked Mary or the co-worker what was wrong, although quiet speculation took place. "Probably [the co-worker]'s messed up again. That Mary knows what's what, so."

Soon after Mary's conversation ended, Mary's boss came in. She quickly looked over the organization of the sale, complimented Mary on how well everything looked, and left. Conversation between the mothers and the workers continued. When Mary was involved in the chat, she discussed school issues and Christmas bother. Families and husbands were not mentioned in this venue.

Although Mary is well known in this school, and it is known that she has a husband and children, Mary did not mention her family while working the jumble sale. Calling upon the status "worker" for Mary means that her personal life is held in abeyance. This may also be because everyone who attended the jumble sale knows the particulars of Mary's life, as indeed they know the particulars of each other's lives. No discussion is necessary—in fact, it may be a relief to be able to interact among adults talking about adult issues.

Mary's separation of the status "worker" from her status as "mother," however, is not as clear-cut as it may appear. Mary appears professional, businesslike, and unemotional in general. She uses understandings about appropriate status behavior with her family and at work. Mary believes that revealing very much at work would be harmful to her position, sometimes because she hears information about other parents:

> You know the way, a lot of the time parents like will come in and they'd tell me things about the home life or what the children would do, or I'd just know a child's particular home situation, and I wouldn't talk about that. I would with my boss, of course, she has to know that sort of thing. But I wouldn't talk to the others about it. Not even the teachers. I'd keep those confidences . . . so parents will come into the community room at school and they'll tell me things. I hear all kinds of stories.

Mary's position reinforces her belief that she should reveal very little to anyone. She is the repository of details about abuse, drug use, alcoholism, and financial difficulties and refuses to gossip about other families.

Like Jeanne, Mary also will not gossip about herself. She articulates categories and depth of detail about which she will talk with coworkers:

> Sex, I wouldn't talk about sex with them. I mean, maybe I'd say "he thought he was a little bit of all right last night" and laugh,

but I wouldn't go into details. Sex is between the two people only. But some of the girls, they'll go into detail about what he did and how he did it and how many times. And I just won't do that. It's no one's business except mine and Joe's. But I'd make a joke of it sometimes. Just no details. And I wouldn't talk about rows, not in detail. Maybe about how we're redecorating, or about the kids, or about the principal or like that. Just not personal stuff like.

Mary keeps a certain distance between herself and her co-workers; however, this distance is not specific to work. Mary uses similar understandings about how a person properly behaves in many areas of her life.

This is demonstrated in interaction with her children. Mary treats her children, as she does many people, in a businesslike way. On a shopping trip to Dublin's City Centre, Mary took two of her three children to a department store bedecked with *The Lion King* movie merchandise. The children's eyes were immediately caught by the Lion King paraphernalia in the children's clothes department. They each had a pound to spend, and it was burning a hole in their pockets. They both lingered over the kitsch, and Paul let out a small whoop: he found a five-pound note on the floor.

Mary shook her head in amazement. "He's always doing that. He always finds money. One time we were in Mary Street [on the north side of the City Centre] and he found a ten-pound note. He's uncanny that way." She allowed him to keep it, with the proviso that he would share two pounds of it with his brother and sister, and put a pound in the savings bank. All the while, Emily was pawing through the Lion King stuff, deciding that she wanted to get a drawing pad kit. "We'll get it on the way out," Mary said firmly. "Ah, Mam, I want it now!" Emily wailed. "No," Mary insisted, "we'll get it on the way out." "No, now!" Emily pouted. She threw a little temper tantrum right there, but Mary ignored it, as did the other shoppers. She looked through clothing, smiling with embarrassment at the store clerks, until Emily was done. Later, Mary did return to the display with Emily and Emily bought her pad.

Once the temper tantrum was over, Mary took the children for a treat in the cafeteria of the department store. The children finished their food quickly, and Mary sat and smoked cigarettes, not talking much with the children. Paul asked whether he could go look at the toys just across the aisle, and Emily asked too. Mary said, "All right, but stay where I can see you." And they did. Mary talked about the children, frustrated at their poking each other all the time but then proudly proclaiming, "but they'd be protecting too. If anyone bothered Paul, Emily would take them on. And vice versa. But they can't seem to leave each other alone. They're always at each other." Mary then brought the children out of the department store, found them some lunch, and walked through the crowded City Centre with them for two hours or so, when it was time for another treat at an ice-cream parlor.

Mary's interaction with her children in the City Centre consisted of correction and providing food and treats. Mary knew that a good mother will have children who behave perfectly—that is, quietly, demurely, without irritation or need of adult companionship. Mary's interaction with her children suggests that her businesslike, nonrevelatory demeanor crosses status expectations. As with her co-workers, Mary does not chat with her children about herself or initiate chat with the children about their activities. In contrast to Jeanne's sociable parental style, Mary's mothering is more traditionally Irish, centering on physical needs and correction rather than conversation or cuddling.

Mary maintains the private aspects of mothering—providing for physical needs and listening rather than actively probing for information—in her work relationships. She uses understandings about proper behavior for herself in most social interactions. These data demonstrate that mothering behavior and work behavior consist of understandings that cross domains. Rather than having one set of understandings that guide behavior as a mother and a wholly different set of understandings that influence behavior at work, Mary uses common understandings of motivation and behavior in what are conventionally thought of as separate social arenas.

IRENE GRAFTON

Irene Grafton is in her late forties, married for twenty-two years with six children. Irene's husband is a bus driver, while Irene works in the home, living in a middle-class area in the south part of Dublin. Irene is short, somewhat stocky, with short gray permed hair. A warm, intelligent woman, Irene uses her experiences and understandings about family life to interpret and act on political, Church, and neighborhood issues. She is most concerned at present with education and training her children.

Irene disagrees with the notion that women are naturally nurturant and men are naturally aggressive. She says that some mothering skills have to be learned:

But I don't think mothering is natural, not at all. I had to learn how to do it. Like for example I had to learn to breast-feed. It didn't come naturally to me, not at all. For the first three it didn't work to breast-feed, I just couldn't do it. The nurses would be hovering and telling me what to do and I just couldn't do it. For the fourth one, I pushed the nurse out the door—and she didn't like that too well—and said I'll do it meself. And I did, and I was able to breast-feed the last three. But I had to really work at it, it wasn't just there for the taking. I mean, you can see the same thing in Africa, when Nestlé's brought in that powder stuff for feeding babies—African women can't breast-feed any more naturally than I could, they have to be taught.

Irene disputes the "naturalness" of at least some maternal behaviors and uses her understandings and experiences to comprehend economic and political issues in different place. She is using some parts of "private" understandings regarding mothering to discuss "public," political issues. Here, Irene discusses her own trouble with learning how to breast-feed to interpret the issues surrounding Nestlé's mismanagement of the marketing of powdered formula in Africa. It is also interesting to note that it took Irene four births to override the authority of the nursing sister, in part demonstrating the Irish difficulty with challenging authority.

Irene apparently has had little difficulty with other parts of maternal behavior that she sees as important. She declares that one of the most important parts of mothering is love, which can be seen through being demonstrative. Irene also thinks that promoting education is crucial to parenting:

Education is really a passport in life. I mean, really, we want the children to work at school. It's expected that you'll do your best. You don't have to be brilliant, but school reports should be good. When they are good, we'll say "well done." It's really about discipline, isn't it, it shows that you're working your way through things, and it should help you learn respect for the teacher. The school report will show all of that. Our kids do pretty well.

Irene encourages her children to do well in school, seeing that as one of her major jobs as a mother. Further, the understanding regarding maternal responsibility to educate has resulted in Irene's involvement in parent-teacher organizations. Irene works on educational issues beyond her children's school, as her association attempts to influence public policy for the whole of the Republic. This shows that Irene has transferred her beliefs about a mother's job to a more public venue, a blend of public and private.

Irene's case deals primarily with ideal understandings, as no data regarding her interaction with children or the education association is available except through thirdhand sources. However, her use of maternal understandings and experiences in other, "public" arenas of public policy shows that aspects of the "private" status of mother are used in social domains other than the private.

NIAMH RILEY

Niamh, 32, has been married to Padraig for ten years; they have two children, aged five and two. Padraig is a builder. Niamh's mother, Siobhan, who has a "little problem" with the drink, lives with the family. The family members teeter between violence, withdrawal, chaos, and, occasionally, normalcy. Usually I met Niamh and Siobhan (and the children) at larger pub sessions, and Padraig would join us once in a while. However, I was invited to the house many times as well. A meal was offered usually, but frequently only whiskey appeared.

Niamh's house was ramshackle inside and out. The little patch of grass in front of her semidetached house served as extra parking, and scraps of paper littered the hedgerow and fence. Curtains and draperies hung askew in the front window facing the street. Inside, children's toys and clothing were scattered in the hallway; coats were draped on the banister. The hallway was usually chillier than the rest of the house, and doors to the parlor, the sitting room, and the kitchen were kept closed to keep the heat in.

My friend Mae and I visited one Sunday morning and were led in to the sitting room. Niamh's mother Siobhan rose from her armchair next to the blaring television, greeting everyone warmly and remarking on the horrible rain lashing down. Holding a cigarette, with ash dangling precariously, Siobhan immediately ordered Niamh to get everyone a drink. Protests that noon was too early for a tumbler full of whiskey were waved away imperiously. Niamh drew her lips into a barely perceptible frown and left to get glasses.

The sitting room was crowded with furniture. A dining table stood near the door of the small room, in front of a new breakfront. The table was already laid for Sunday dinner; mismatched chairs ranged around the table. On the mantel above the fireplace stood beer cans and wine bottles, some empty and some with candles crudely stuck in their openings. Newspapers, empty beer and soda cans, cigarette butts, and paper plates were scattered in the apparently unused grate. Siobhan returned to her chair, slumped, crossed her legs, and clutched her half-full glass of whiskey. Her overflowing ashtray sat on one arm of the chair, and her glass of whiskey on the other. Opposite the armchair, next to the fireplace, we sat on an overstuffed sofa.

Niamh returned with tumblers and put them on the table, moving a place setting out of the way. She then sat on the sofa, sliding down to slump. Niamh was wearing a bathrobe, while Siobhan was in a smart knit suit and pearls. While everyone in the room chain-smoked, the children and Padraig flitted in and out of the room. Padraig was cooking the dinner, asking Niamh somewhat testily for instructions.

The children were dressed in pajamas and slippers; they hadn't had their morning wash-up, and their faces were covered in chocolate, jam, and dirt. The younger child had also managed to smear chocolate across her pajama top. The older child was cleaner, with combed hair and a decidedly responsible air about her. The older girl continually asked the visitors whether they needed anything. Every time she did so, Niamh scolded her for bothering her guests; within a minute, however, Niamh asked her to fetch various items. This hints at an interesting mixture of public and private role relationships: since company had come calling, children should be more docile than they would be otherwise. However, because Niamh knew her guests rather well, her immediate scolding response to her child's "helpfulness" was tempered by more private understandings about motherhood. She could reward her child's wish to be helpful; she simply had trouble coordinating her judgment of the private and public elements guiding the interaction and social situation.[7] The role relationships of "friend–friend" influenced, in part and at first, a set of understandings with more public elements about how a child should behave with strangers. The same role relationships, however, elicited understandings with more private dimensions concerning how a child may behave at home among familiar people.[8]

Most of the visit revolved around my Irish friend Mae, who is a master storyteller. Her tales, humorous, long, and at least likely to be partially true, involved her sons and daughter and all the disastrous ways they have tried to "help" her. Later, she told me that she was trying to defuse the tension that she felt in the house. The sheer force of her personality and the delivery of her stories did seem to have a relaxing effect on Niamh, Padraig, and Siobhan. At the least, once Mae begins telling stories, there is no stopping her. She went on for about forty-five minutes, as Padraig cleaned up the children, dressed them, and combed their hair, in preparation for one o'clock Mass. As Mae told her stories, Siobhan nodded off now and then, cigarette in hand more or less near the ashtray. Siobhan would startle awake, start humming in a delicate soprano, and occasionally would burst into song. Padraig brought the children back into the sitting room, and the girls commenced riding their tricycles in the sitting room. Niamh very sharply reprimanded them. She then told Padraig to take the trikes out to the hall. He shot her a venomous look and took the children and the trikes out to the hallway.

The children's improved appearance was a signal for Mae to leave. She had finished her whiskey and announced that it was time to be going. We got into her car and left. Mae discussed Niamh and Padraig with no prompting, saying that they were having marital problems. Siobhan is also a constant worry. "But they're all grand people really, and that Niamh would do anything for yeh, give yeh her last penny," Mae said, defending her friends. "They'll work it out, I think. It's just a rough patch right now, but Siobhan's going to go to the sisters' home [for treatment of alcoholism]."

Mae only very obliquely made it known that she was well aware of the tensions in the house. In her role relationship with Niamh of "friend–friend," Niamh's mothering was not a topic of conversation either with Niamh or with me. Instead, Mae defended her friend, although I offered no attack, and she believed that her friend would work out her problems. Niamh's status as "mother" was not particularly relevant to the friendship except as a fact. The content of Mae's stories had to do with motherhood, but they were offered in support of the friend Niamh, not only the mother Niamh.

Niamh's interaction with her friends and with her family show the interesting blend of public and private understandings. Elements of public and private understandings came into play as she disciplined her child. At first, gauging the situation to be more public than it was, Niamh scolded her child. She then realized that she could use more private understandings with her little girl; she reoriented her comprehension of the social situation and role relationships as being more private. Mae encouraged this through telling stories of her bold children, with the result that she subtly offered advice and comfort to Niamh. At the same time, Mae's stories are famous in her network to be just a little fantastic and exaggerated; this knowledge very likely partly shaped the reception of the stories, advice, and comfort.

Mae's stories of motherhood also demonstrate the interpenetration of public and private elements of cultural understandings. One aim of the stories was to provide Niamh with some emotional support; this was a more private concern, associated with friendship. However, another purpose was to entertain an audience—a goal connected with more public understandings about proper social behavior. Mae walked a very thin line in this social situation with no little delicacy. Her behavior and Niamh's show that an interaction usually contains a mixture of elements of public and private understandings.

MOTHERHOOD AND ASPECTS OF THE PRIVATE

The cases of Jeanne O'Brien, Mary Evans, Irene Grafton, and Niamh Riley show that mothers in Ireland use understandings about family life and the status "mother" in social situations beyond the family. Jeanne O'Brien successfully applied her maternal experience to a sensitive work situation. Mary Evans behaves in a consistent way across social domains, using similar understandings about appropriate behavior regardless of the social situation. Irene Grafton has used her maternal experience to become politically involved in public policy issues. Niamh Riley flexibly adjusts her expectations and understandings about proper social behavior after judging how much publicness and how much privateness she should blend. All four women demonstrate that the status "mother" is not a solely private status.

All four women also defy the Church's ideal understandings regarding the responsibilities of mothers. The Church insists that women should concern themselves primarily with their families. Jeanne, Mary, and Irene are involved in activities outside the domestic arena and take pride in those activities, while Niamh expects her husband to clean, cook, and care for the children at least part of the time.

At the same time, Jeanne, Mary, Irene, and Niamh meet some of the other ideal understandings surrounding the behavior of mothers. Mary in particular is strong and unemotional, tending to her children's physical needs but rarely initiating physically comforting or sociable behaviors. Jeanne, on the other hand, chats with her children and is physically affectionate as she begins to change some ideal understandings regarding motherhood. Irene reports that she is demonstrative and that she believes her daughters see her as a friend. Niamh displays some characteristically Irish mothering patterns. The four women use some of the ideal understandings concerning motherhood in their everyday behavior, although they do not adopt all of them.

Mothers in Ireland negotiate a complex mixture of ideal understandings regarding their behaviors in public and in private. Fathers, too, must find their way through Irish expectations for men. It is to Irish fathers that I turn next.

NOTES

1. Interestingly, Irish women seem to agree with the Church. In 1987, women made up only 32.4% of the labor force (*European Communities Encyclopedia and Directory* 1992: 136).

2. It will be remembered that Irish voters passed, by a fraction of a percentage point, an amendment to this article in which divorce would be allowed in specific and limited circumstances. In February 1998, after a series of failed legal challenges to the 1995 divorce referendum, Article 40.3.2 was changed to read:

A court designated by law may grant of a dissolution of marriage where, but only where, it is satisfied that—i. at the date of the institution of the proceedings, the spouses have lived apart from one another for a period of, or periods amounting to, at least four years in the last five years, ii. there is no reasonable prospect of a reconciliation between the spouses, iii. such provision as the Court considers proper having regard to the circumstances exists or will be made for the spouses, any children of either or both of them and any other person prescribed by law, and iv. any further conditions prescribed by law are complied with. [sic] (http//www.maths.tcd.ie/pub/Constitution/Articles40–44.html)

The amendment approved by voters specified a four-year waiting period after separation before a divorce action could be filed. It was otherwise similar to the defeated 1986 amendment, in which a judge must determine that a marriage has failed irrevocably before granting spousal and child financial support (Dillon 1993:1; Irish Consulate, Chicago, personal communication).

3. Whiting and Edwards (1988) argue that their data from Liberia, Kenya, India, Mexico, the Philippines, Okinawa, and the United States show three basic "maternal styles" (Whiting and Edwards 1988:93–117). The "training mother" teaches her young children responsibility and obedience through showing children how to garden, look after animals, and take care of the house (Whiting and Edwards 1988:94). The "controlling mother" tries to dominate her children rather than teach the children specific tasks: "they frequently reprimand after the fact rather than advising their children what to do beforehand" [sic] (Whiting and Edwards 1988:112). The "sociable mother" values pleasant interaction with her children; interaction is "characterized by relatively high levels of information exchange and other kinds of reciprocal, friendly interaction" (Whiting and Edwards 1988:113).

4. Loughane (1983) did not observe family interaction or behavior outside the home. She interviewed women in their homes but did not observe behaviors. It can be assumed that Loughane's data, then, reveal ideal understandings rather than actual behaviors.

5. "Love" and "comfort" are demonstrated through a mother's sacrifices for her children. It does not typically include much cuddling, sociable conversation, or opinion elicitation, at least by mothers over thirty years old. Scheper-Hughes notes that babies in Kerry in the 1970s were rarely breast-fed, rocked, or held (Scheper-Hughes 1979:145–146). I observed the same pattern in 1990s Dublin. Despite this, most informants reported that they felt loved and cared for by their mothers.

6. As will be seen in Chapter 7, women see men as little more than children, useless around the house and of little help in rearing the family.

7. Scheper-Hughes (1979) characterizes similar kinds of Irish parent–child interactions as "double-binding," in that two conflicting demands are made, creating an intolerable problem (Scheper-Hughes 1979:166). Niamh's behavior with her child could be seen as double-binding, in that she presents two different messages: do not be helpful but be helpful. I have seen this pattern used by many Irish mothers. For instance, I attended a party during which an eight-year-old girl cuddled close to me. Her mother scolded her severely for being so familiar with me, even though I knew the family quite well and even though I did not mind the child's presence. The mother pulled the child up off the floor where she was sitting next to me, causing a glass of soda to fall over. The mother furiously asked the girl: "Now what yeh are?" The girl mumbled something I could not hear. The mother loudly said, "Yeh, that's right, you're an eejit, a bleedin' eejit, spilling that Coke all over!" The mother then hugged the child close. That seems to be a clear if extreme example of double-binding.

8. I should note, however, that this entire interaction was underlain with a diffuse sense of hostility; there was an undercurrent of anger among the adult members of the family.

CHAPTER 7

He's Another Child Really

The family, although not the father, is particularly important to Irish people. Fathers are meant to provide economic support and little else in most Irish families. As shown in Chapter 6, *Bunreacht na hÉireann* (the Irish Constitution) declares, in Article 41, that the family is the cornerstone of Irish society. However, as noted in Chapter 6, only mothers and women (the terms are used interchangeably) are discussed in the Constitution. Fathers do not appear in the Constitution, which may reflect an Irish belief that a father is not as crucial an element in Irish family life as a mother. Indeed, Nancy Scheper-Hughes points out that mothers in the village she studied in rural Kerry excluded fathers from child rearing (Scheper-Hughes 1979:147–148). As will be seen, some urban fathers also leave child rearing to their wives. Although some recent court cases have begun to bring fathers into the family legally—specifically in terms of child support, the rights of unmarried fathers, and paternity leave—Irish cultural understandings of "father" remain somewhat contradictory.

Besides the legal and constitutional exclusion of "father" as fundamental to family life, the massive social changes that have occurred in Irish society in the past ten or so years have resulted in two different sets of understandings regarding fatherhood, so that the "traditional" and the "new man" fathers are discussed as if they contain almost completely opposite sets of understandings. These understandings, further, are almost mutually exclusive. Men have trouble negotiating their behavior through traditional and "new man" statuses; this is complicated by the large number of marital separations and, to a lesser extent, divorces, that have only lately begun to be acknowledged politically, legally, and religiously.

Finally, it is difficult to separate the status "father" from the status "husband." This is partly because Irish men are not considered full adults until they have produced a child; working full-time seems to have nothing to do with becoming an "adult."[1] Marriage itself does not constitute a promotion to adulthood, although it is considered an appropriate and morally required step. Many Dubliners do not seem to consider the marital relationship to be as important as is parenthood. Failing to fulfill the requirements of one status—"husband"—seems to automatically precipitate an experience of failing to fulfill the requirements for the other—"father." Given the rate of marital breakdown and the high rate of unemployment, many Irish men are experiencing themselves as failures.

Regardless of these issues, however, there do seem to be two different sets of understandings concerning the status "father." One, which informants call "traditional," appears to be more dominant in working-class and rural families, though it is represented in middle-class families as well. The other, emergent ideal father is what is referred to, usually mockingly, as the "new man," and this form seems to appear only in the educated middle classes. The "new man" has not shown up in rural Ireland yet.

In this chapter, I discuss ideal understandings concerning Irish fatherhood. Several fathers are presented. The difficulties that these fathers encounter as they try to use ideal understandings to guide behavior with their children, wives (or ex-wives), and employers will be shown. It will be seen that Irish fathers employ understandings and expectations concerning their "public" and "private" lives more subtly than Irish mothers do. Fathers use understandings surrounding fatherhood in other role relationships, but that use is more particularized, whereas mothers' use is more generalized and overt. In addition, men are not as clear as mothers are about their status responsibilities in using such understandings, and fathers seem to have strong conflicts about their self-worth and the nature of their masculinity. In contrast, women appear fairly secure in their statuses and role relationships.

IDEAL UNDERSTANDINGS OF IRISH FATHERHOOD— THE "TRADITIONAL" FATHER

Perhaps the most important cultural understanding influencing behavior is that the "traditional" Irish father is the breadwinner, the provider for the family. The father should be able to bring home the bacon, whether the bacon is a paycheck or a welfare check. Given the 13% unemployment rate, higher in the working-class sector, many fathers struggle to fill these expectations adequately. Some Irish men believe that this aspect of fatherhood is based on a natural division of labor dictated by biological differences between men and women. These men say that what they describe as male physical superiority and naturally aggressive nature leads to men's superior adaptation to the business world. Women, in this view, work only if they have to or if they do not have children to take care of. Women are naturally nurturing and only fulfilled through children; men do not have the natural capacities to nurture children. It is sensible, to these men, that they should be the ones working or drawing the dole if unemployed, leaving the bulk of child rearing to their wives. Previous ethnographers have noted this pattern as well, both in rural and urban areas (Arensberg and Kimball 1968 [1940]:48; Humphreys 1966:124; Scheper-Hughes 1979:148; Loughane 1983:132).

A family, then, in the "traditional" worldview, consists of family members using a set of complementary rather than symmetrical behaviors. Fathers are "good" fathers if they, and they alone (that is, without mothers working outside the house) are able to meet their families' needs adequately for food, shelter, clothing, and whatever luxuries can be had. Being the family provider is the crucial aspect of being a "father." Associated with this aspect is what happens when the pay packet gets home. A "good" father hands the pay packet, or dole check, to his wife. Complementarity is seen here: the father obtains the living, and the mother runs the household on it. Most Irish men in the "traditional" status do not involve themselves in household finances. As long as the wife gives them a small allowance, they appear to be content. One informant, a young working-class woman, said that a father who tries to control household finances "is generally shunned by whoever it is who finds out about it. At the same time, a man is not expected to hand over all his money to the household and shouldn't be expected to."

The lack of involvement in household financial matters is usually extended to child rearing. Irish traditional fathers are not typically expected to be as involved in day-to-day child care as mothers are. Even if the father is on the dole and therefore around the family home in the daytime, it is the mother who deals with everyday child rearing. The father is the final authority on major discipline or financial issues, but he leaves everyday decisions to "mammy."

One family I knew demonstrates this. The father, "Breandan," is a full-time mature university student (he draws the dole and gets student grants). His wife, "Stephanie," is a university student as well. They have five children, ranging in age from 13 to a newborn; both Breandan and Stephanie are 32. One day I visited with them; Stephanie was out but was expected home shortly. Breandan was in charge of the children. As he and I chatted, the children constantly interrupted us with questions and requests. Although Breandan was very patient with the children, affectionately calling them "pet," "chicken," "love," or "honey," all requests were countered with "wait until Mammy gets home." Most families I encountered in Ireland followed this pattern: Daddy baby-sat but left all decisions—to say nothing of the laundry and washing up—to Mammy.[2]

The division of labor seen so far in financial and child-rearing matters continues with household tasks. Traditional fathers are expected to be responsible for "manly" (informant's description) tasks: taking out the rubbish, repairing the house or car, maintaining the garden, electrical matters, and "outside" (informant's term) work of any kind (compare Yanagisako 1987 regarding Issei marriage tasks). Traditional fathers are not expected to cook, take responsibility for the children (e.g., putting them to bed, making sure they do their schoolwork, supervising their chores), sew, do laundry, clean, make beds, or do the washing up. If somehow they are inveigled into doing such tasks, they see it as and are perceived by family members to be "helping out" rather than performing their specific responsibilities. One young woman, originally from Connemara, related the following story illustrating the nature of "helping out": during Christmas holidays, she and her fiancé were visiting her aunts and uncles. She told me: "My fiancé was doing the wash-up after dinner whilst my dad, uncle, and myself sat for a cup of tea. My uncle told my fiancé to be careful in case he spoilt his future wife." My informant believed that this was an example of how "traditional" fathers interpreted what was women's work and men's work in a family. She thought that her uncle was instructing her fiancé in Irish ideal understandings concerning proper male behavior.

Many women appear uncomfortable if their husbands "take over" "inside" work. Although they complain about how "useless" their husbands are in general, they seem to resent what they see as a subtle criticism should their husbands take on cooking: "He thinks he can do it better," one informant told me. "Of course, he can't, he's hopeless in the kitchen." Traditional fathers would receive scant support for taking on tasks that are not properly theirs, since they would be violating ideal understandings about fatherhood and masculinity.

Some more abstract qualities make up proper "father" behavior. Many men feel "responsible" for their family beyond economic support, though being the breadwinner is the clearest marker of responsibility. Being responsible involves taking a leadership position, directing behavior and teaching common-sense skills such as car repair (usually to their sons only). Traditional fathers only rarely would be comfortable discussing emotional issues or problems with their children (as, ideally, would mothers); they do not play with their young children; and they seem most involved with their children once the children have reached drinking age. It is only when a child, male or female (though most likely male), has reached eighteen that a traditional father will spend time with his child, usually in the pub. Prior to that time, the traditional father sees himself as in charge of the family, the chairman of the board, while his wife is to be the chief operating officer. One middle-class man in his early 40s told me that, while he loved his two teenage children (a boy and girl), he didn't know them very well and didn't really think that was his job. "They seem nice," he said, "but really, that's my wife's area. I bring in a good paycheck so that the kids can get the latest fashions. Besides, they spend most of their time with their friends. I suppose they're nice kids, they don't get into much trouble, but I don't think about it too much." In his professional life, this man has fought for women's rights but is, as he says, "a traditional Irish man" at home.

Some traditional men extend their sense of responsibility to their wives' emotional stability. They see themselves as being more rational than women, and they think that, if they withdrew from the marriage, their wives would go to pieces. One man discussed above, Breandan, demonstrates this. At times he is unhappy with his marriage, but he remains because he is convinced that Stephanie would be unable to cope without his strength. "I feel needed," he says, "and sometimes it feels as though I've six kids and not five." In some ways, traditional fathers experience fatherhood in their relationships with their wives rather than with their children.

It should be noted, however, that many women would dispute this kind of claim made by Breandan and men like him; many women feel that they—and not their husbands—are the ones who hold the family together and that they are mother rather than wife to their husbands. When I discussed Breandan's comment about his wife with a female informant (who did not know Breandan), my informant reprimanded me strongly. "Yeh shouldn't take him too seriously now," she advised me. "I'll bet she organizes everything; there's a million men in Ireland just like him. Don't feel too sorry for him." She went on to say that men put the blame for their problems on what they call the fragility of their wives. Men always say that they would leave their wives if they could, but they do not because they say their wives would fall apart. My informant concluded by saying that men use their wives as an excuse for doing nothing to make their marriages better, and that they're little more than lazy children.

My informant's beliefs are reflected in one rather popular radio advertisement[3] for a candy bar. In this spot, an Irish woman warmly talks about how irresponsible her little one is, the dreadful language he uses, and how he never goes to bed on time. But it's all worth it, she chuckles, when his "little face" lights up at the sight of the candy bar. The ad ends with the woman saying, "Sometimes, though, I wonder why I married him." Though the ad is humorous, it conveys a clear set of Irish understandings about marriage and family life, especially those which present contradictory messages to men. On the one hand, men should be good providers; on the other, men are "useless" children. Regardless of women's assessment of men, the "traditional" father is supposed to support his family economically and is meant to do heavy repairs to house and car—the "outside" work. He is a full adult, however, only when children appear.

IDEAL UNDERSTANDINGS OF IRISH FATHERHOOD— THE "NEW MAN"

"New men" attempt to make the boundary between marital and parental relationships clearer. Expectations surrounding behavior for those occupying the "new man" father status stand in almost complete opposition to those of the "traditional" father. It should be noted first, however, that I have only heard of these men. I have never observed new men as fathers in action in any depth, but rather only in passing. It appears that this is an emergent status and it is only young, middle-class, university-educated men who are apparently adopting these behaviors (some gay men have adopted them as well; however, in general, Irish gay men do not have children). At the same time, mothers whose husbands are traditional say that they wish their husbands would change (even though, as noted earlier, when their husbands try to do so, their efforts are denigrated by their wives). Even though no actual "new men" fathers will be discussed here, it is a status about which I kept hearing during fieldwork. Men would discuss doing housework or cleaning, almost always with the tag line "Of course, I'm no new man." A group of women I came to know screamed with laughter to my queries about whether their husbands were "new men." One married woman in her thirties explained:

C'mere![3] We'd all love to have one of them fellas. They're thin on the ground really but women love 'em. It's the auld fellas who make the fun of them; the auld wans, they're threatened maybe by them. But you'll never find a real new man anywhere; it doesn't exist really. But our fellas, they're trying. They're not good enough [an explosion of laughter from the group] but they *are* men after all!

Although these women, and most female informants, said that they wished their husbands were new men, there is a curious ambivalence, seen in the woman's remarks above denigrating men. Men who adopt some "new men" behaviors apologize for those behaviors. Even though a new set of expectations is growing around this status, significant conflict surrounds it. Still, it is likely that, within a few years, more fathers employing "new man" expectations will appear, at least among the educated, "Dublin 4" middle-class intelligentsia. That there is considerable discussion about this as-yet-unrealized status makes it a salient part of this chapter.

"Sharing" seems to be the keyword for "new men" fathers. A new man and his wife usually have careers (as opposed to jobs), and the new man is expected to share all household-related chores, as well as child care, equally with his wife. If the wife is better at car repair than the husband, then the wife does the car repair. If the husband is a better cook, then he does most of the cooking. A new man helps his children with homework, takes them to the park, plays with them, bathes them, and in general is supposed to be as involved with them on a day-to-day basis as is the mother. Rather than a traditional role relationship of complementarity based on alleged biological—and thus inborn behavioral—differences between the sexes, the new man and his wife structure their relationship of complementarity and symmetry based in general on actual differences in either ability or efficacy.

For example, my informants tell me that, even five years ago, it was almost unheard of to see a man pushing a pram, and it was next to impossible to see a man pushing a pram on his own and enjoying it. These days, however, young men, by themselves, wheel what appear to be expensive prams around the neighborhood on Saturday and Sunday afternoons. They cheerfully are chatting away to their child, commenting on the passing scene in encouraging and friendly tones. These young men are not "baby-sitting" (as opposed to caring for their child). "Baby-sitting" carries with it the implication that the baby-sitter is "helping out" with a task not normally his own; a new man sees child care as his bailiwick as much as his wife's. They also are not separated fathers, as most of them are wearing wedding rings. Rather than leaving all child rearing to the mother, the new man actively participates in child care, often on his own as he interacts with his child much more than a traditional father would.

"New men" fathers, then, seem to share few of the traditional understandings of fatherhood. It is likely that their own fathers were traditional, but the many changes in values and morals in the last ten years in Irish society seem to have helped create this new way of being a father. I suspect that these changes have extended to marital relationships. New men appear to expect to have a different kind of marriage than the older generation has had. Foremost is a concentration on the marital relationship, which does not seem to obtain either in the older generations or in traditional marriages. New men and their wives appear to take the marriage as seriously as they do their children, and they also seem to draw a more definite boundary around the marital relationship, seeing it as separate from the parental relationship. This is a clear difference between new men and traditional fathers. The latter do not appear to differentiate between marital and parental statuses as the new men do. Marital understandings and relationships will be discussed more fully in Chapter 8.

MARITAL BREAKDOWN AND FATHERHOOD

A complicating factor in looking at family statuses is the growing rate of marital breakdown. It is almost always the mother who has custody of children when a marriage breaks down[4], and the father, regardless of how deep his interest in his children is, simply has less involvement in his children's lives. The mother and father usually live in separate places (though not always); the mother and children typically remain in the family home and the father either returns to his family of origin, rooms with a new partner, friends, or siblings, or finds a small bedsit.[5]

A father's sense of responsibility is challenged when the marriage breaks down. He cannot provide for his family as well as he had before the separation, since he must support two households rather than one. If he wishes to be involved in his child's life, it is more difficult to do so, particularly if the relationship with the mother is not very good. He generally does not receive much emotional support from his parents and siblings as a newly single man. Although some families are supportive, the separated men with whom I worked said that their parents, and their mothers in particular, continually pressured the men to repair their broken marriages. Unless a man's wife has behaved very badly—through a series of affairs, for example—the mothers of separated men discourage any discussion of how or why the marriage failed. A separated man's mother usually also discourages the separated man from dating. It is nearly impossible for a man to enter into a new marriage in the Republic at the current time since divorce is very difficult to obtain. In addition, divorce carries with it immense social disapproval. A father receives little sympathy for the emotional fallout from a failed marriage, reflecting a wider Irish understanding regarding the perceived selfishness of the expression of emotion (see Chapter

8). Generally a father in such a situation has many unresolved problems that he brings into a new relationship, and, given the lack of divorce until very recently, is often tempted to try to repair the broken marriage rather than moving on. A traditional father in particular finds it difficult to be a father and not a husband.

SÉAMÁS QUINN

Séamás Quinn is a 45-year-old separated father of two. A highly placed civil servant, Séamás is middle class, well educated, and well traveled. Of average Irish male height (5'7"), he is bespectacled and balding, with a gently teasing manner and a quick smile. Séamás sees his daughters every weekend and at least once during the week. After his separation, Séamás moved in with his sister's family, where his mother was living in the house as well; he also saw a psychologist during this time, an unusual choice for an Irish person. Only recently has Séamás bought and moved into his own apartment, the first place he has lived on his own. Séamás continues to bring his laundry over to his mother, however: "She'd be hurt if I didn't. Really! But I do my own ironing!"

One part of Séamás's story illustrates the complexity of public and private for Irish men and fathers. It is also interesting to note that Séamás chose this story to tell after he and I discussed the theoretical background of this study. Séamás, in his words, "fell apart" when his marriage disintegrated some four years ago. He found himself unable to concentrate at work. Just before it was apparent that his supervisor was going to call him in, Séamás confided in his boss. Although he provided few details, he says that he gave his boss the bare bones of his "situation." Almost immediately, his supervisor detailed him for a six-month overseas assignment, telling Séamás that it might do him some good to get away from the "situation." While Séamás views himself as having been competent to carry out the overseas assignment— it was not given to him purely out of personal concern on the part of his boss—he also believes that his supervisor saw his personal pain and searched for a way to help him. Rather than giving Séamás a two-week holiday to sort everything out, his supervisor found him a place drastically away from his problems. Séamás views his overseas time as valuable, growth-producing, and ultimately helpful, though, he says wryly, "I didn't do much for my department while I was there."

A personal crisis and the painful adjustment to new statuses of separated father and single person led a supervisor in a seemingly rationalistic bureaucracy to respond with a therapeutic solution rather than a heartless one. Séamás retained his dignity as a worker, though he was aware that his boss was going out of his way to be personally helpful as the separation went on. The public arena of work was deeply affected by a personal "situation." Séamás and his supervisor altered their mainly simplex role relationship of "supervisor–worker" as private elements were discussed and used to effect a significant change in Séamás's life. Public and private interact here in complex ways.

Séamás also finds himself affected—"interrupted"—by his daughters at work, as the older girl attends a secondary school directly across the street from his office. He feels guilty for becoming irritated with the interruptions:

> Well, she's a cute[6] one all right. She came in bold as brass the other day. "Daddy, daddy, I've lost me bus fare." And this in the middle of a phone call to Saudi Arabia. "And I'm so hungry too." She took five quid off me just like that. I couldn't turn her away, really, could I? But I gave her a bit of a talking to later on. The Saudis think we're too indulgent as it is with our girls, me especially, and this Saudi could hear the whole thing.

Séamás finds himself negotiating a business relationship influenced in part by how he treats his daughters. The role relationship father–daughter is altered depending on the social arena in which Séamás and his daughter find themselves. At the office, Séamás wants to be rid of her, while at home he has plenty of time for her. Similarly, the role relationship Irish civil servant–Saudi civil servant is modified when Séamás's status as father is part of the picture.

PAUL RAFTERY

Paul Raftery is also a civil servant, frequently working with Saudis and Omanis. Paul is 38, quite short, balding, and mustachioed. Like Séamás, he is separated. He has a nine-year-old boy, whom he sees very often. Paul also sees his ex-wife frequently. They attend parties as a married couple and in many ways are regarded as still fully married, although Paul reports that they do not have sex. Paul's ties with his wife would seem to reflect Paul's ambivalence about his separation. Unlike Séamás, Paul is not well educated and worked his way up from a utility lineman position to his current job as a marketing manager for a semistate utility.

Although he now considers himself to be middle class, in many ways Paul uses working-class understandings to shape his world. He firmly believes that men and women have significant biological differences that determine behavior, a belief that obtains mainly among my working-class informants. Paul is also ambivalent about being separated but refuses to find a psychotherapist, despite the repeated entreaties of his friends. His friends say that they have been listening to his complaints and excuses about his ex-wife for four years now and that Paul really ought to be moving on. Paul feels that a psychotherapist is for those who are weak of will and that psychotherapy will not do any good. Among working-class informants, Paul's attitudes about psychotherapy are commonplace. Psychotherapy, to them, is an American invention that forgives bad behavior and which is selfish to boot, since you sit and pay someone to listen to you and you alone for an hour.

Finally, Paul's working-class understandings are seen in the way he structures his workday. Although most people arrive at his office by 9:00 A.M., Paul comes in around 9:30 or 10:00. After checking in, Paul goes down the street for breakfast, returning in half an hour to 45 minutes. Paul then works until 11:00 A.M., when the office takes a fifteen-minute tea break; it often stretches to half an hour. Once the coffee break is over, Paul works until 1:00 P.M., when he takes a lunch break. This one to one and a half-hour break involves a full dinner and a few pints. Once lunch is over, Paul works some more and usually leaves the office around 4:30 or 5:00 P.M. Paul's relaxed attitude toward work is only a little unusual among Irish workers; particularly among laborers and builders, the "tea break" can extend for long periods of time as long as the boss is not looking. Paul justifies his workday on the basis of his hard work as a lineman; he believes that he has earned the right to take it easy now. He further says that his thrice-yearly trips to the Middle East make up for his shorter days in Dublin.

However, as I was leaving Ireland, Paul and his workmates told me, separately, that Paul's supervisors were beginning to question whether Paul was earning his salary, since sales in his department were plummeting. This was particularly true with the arrival of a new secretary who "works too hard," Rosemary, Paul's secretary, told me. "Yeh see," Rosemary said, leaning over confidentially, "she works through tea breaks and lunch breaks. It's just too much." Paul agreed strongly: "Yeah, it's too much. We don't work that way and, I'll be honest, it's worrying." Paul saw the situation as dangerous: "Yeh just don't know who she knows. She's been with the company for thirteen years; she may be reporting back to people and we wouldn't even know it. She might have connections with people at different levels, and she hasn't been around our team long enough to understand how we work. She might tell other people without knowing that we don't work the way she does. She just works too hard." Paul's comments reflect the mixture of public and private dimensions of his team. When a new workmate seemed not to share understandings about appropriate work behavior, Paul and Rosemary became nervous. Paul showed a heightened awareness of the different role relationships involved. He and Rosemary shared a "friend–friend" role relationship more than anything else; that role relationship involved far more private elements concerning friendship behavior than public elements regarding work behavior. The new workmate had established a "workmate–workmate" role relationship relatively quickly, from Paul's account. She did not, apparently, share Paul's understanding that family and other personal concerns were more important than work concerns. Further, the fact that the new workmate was an unknown quantity frightened Paul. He worried that his workplace role relationships might become less warm, taking on more public elements of work understandings. The arrival of a new secretary in the midst of firm role relationships based on more private elements than public ones created a small crisis for Paul, and for Rosemary, demonstrating that public and private understandings blend in significant ways.

Paul's connections to the Middle East also show the complexity of his public and private relationships. His status as father in particular has been crucial to building some business relationships with his Omani colleagues. So Paul carries photographs of his son in his wallet and shows them often. The photos, Paul thinks, show his devotion and solidity as a family man; the fact of his failed marriage is less salient to his Omani colleagues than the fact of his fatherhood. In fact, on a recent business trip, Paul brought his son with him. When his Omani colleagues have visited Ireland, Paul ensured that they spent a good deal of time with his son (although Paul's ex-wife was never invited). Paul uses several different role relationships in his business life: father–son, father–father (with business colleagues), worker–supervisor, friend–friend.

In fact, Paul has been testing the friend–friend role relationship lately with his erratic appearance. His secretary reports that she is becoming tired of covering for him. "Well, really," Rosemary says flatly, "I'm lying for him and I'll tell yeh now that me own job is not all that secure. I've told him I won't be doing it for that much longer!" Paul had not changed his behavior at the time I left, despite his worries about the new workmate. Paul is employing the friend–friend role relationship in an increasingly inappropriate way at work, according to Rosemary. He could be seen as employing a role relationship that is dysfunctional for an adult in a work situation: errant child–stern mother. He does seem to expect forgiveness and understanding regardless of his behavior. His friends seem to provide that.

Paul, then, demonstrates both the successful and the sometimes dysfunctional blending of public and private role relationships. He employs aspects of his "father" status in his business dealings. He also seems to employ more childish statuses in structuring his business day.

JOE EVANS

Joe Evans is 38, an unemployed painter with three children. He says that "I would be working class if I was working!" His wife, Mary, is unemployed as well; we met Mary in Chapter 6. Both are enrolled in FÁS schemes. Both Mary and Joe work in schools, Mary as an administrative aide in the mornings and Joe as a school custodian in the afternoons. Joe stands about 5'8", with a shock of thick, curly black hair and blue eyes. Joe is perhaps fifteen pounds overweight. He is voluble and charming, with clear and usually well-informed opinions about a range of domestic and foreign issues. He is active in local parents' organizations.

Joe has been unemployed for a good part of his adult life. When his oldest boys, Michael and Paul (now 12 and 8), were infants, Mary worked as a cleaner in a hospital in the City Centre and Joe cared for the children:

> *Joe*: When we first started living here, I looked after Michael for a good while when he was a baby.
>
> *Mary*: Which you did! 'Cause I was working. That's right.
>
> *Joe*: Because Mary was working, so I was here. But, em, I used to bring him up and down to the creche [day-care center], 'cause the creche was only starting up there. And people used to see me with a pram. And then it was, "God, there's a man with a pram and a baby. Isn't he very good?" And there could be sympathy, and you were looked at as a creature going up the road pushing a pram, very much so.

Although Joe looked like a "new man," he did not feel that way. He notes here that people thought it was extraordinary for a man to push a baby carriage or to be caring for children in the neighborhood in broad daylight. However, Joe did not meet the ideal understandings surrounding the "traditional" father; he was not employed and was not providing for his family economically as well as he would like to be doing. At the same time, "new man" understandings were not common currency even six to eight years ago. Joe was aware of being judged as weird and "very good" for caring for his children. Joe rejects the "new man" set of understandings for himself.

Instead, Joe has clear, "traditional" ideas about how to be a father. Mary and Joe discuss Emily, the six-year-old daughter. Emily is, in their eyes, too "cute" for her own good. Mary and Joe describe Emily's general personality in some specific terms:

Mary: Emily's the one who won't get up and let someone sit in her seat in the bus.

E.A.T.: Oh? Will she not?

Mary: No. I've had rows with her in the bus trying to get her to give the seat to an older lady or something like that. But now she knows I'll just lift her up and put her on me lap.

Joe: And she'll have a long face and a moan.

Mary: I nearly died at her carry-on.

Joe: She'll carry on.

Mary: Oh, she really did, she carried on, it was disgraceful. The thing is now she won't do like that in front of her daddy!

Joe: Well, she knows that her daddy will just grab her by the scruff of her neck and pull her. Yet . . . now . . . I say this boastfully and I don't mean it in a domineering or bullying way. But when I say to my kids "jump," I expect them to say "how high?" And until they're eighteen years of age, I rule them. When they are eighteen years of age, they walk out that door, making a living for themselves, anytime after they're eighteen . . . I'd shag [throw] them out, you must be joking!

Joe expects, like any good "traditional" father, that his children will respect him and that they will obey him unquestioningly. Joe, along with Mary, goes on to describe how he treats his children as he uses his understandings about proper traditional father behavior:

Joe: We don't sound too bad, but there are times when we give out to our kids. All the time. All the time.

Mary: Yeh, all the time, I'll give out to them.

Joe: We give them, we give them very negative vibes all the time. There are times that I feel that. We're forever giving out to [yelling at] them, telling them to wash their face: "you should know how to wash your face. You should be doing the washing of the face." Sometimes I have doubts about that. If you continually—the child who lives with criticism grows up to be—

Mary: We try to be saying to them, yeh don't have to be telling them every morning to wash their face. They know they have to do it.

Joe: Yeah, but they don't. So yeh have to tell them. Then you're back again.

E.A.T.: Yeah, but . . . is there a difference between saying "you should know how to wash your face" and saying "you're so dirty, you're an eejit" [idiot]?

Mary: Oh, yeah, yeah, yeah (loudly).

Joe: Oh, yes, yeah (loudly).

Mary: Yeah, yeh can't keep on saying that.

Joe: No, occasionally though they will get that. Certainly from me they will get that. And it's sharp, and I shouldn't be saying that. (Whispering) I shouldn't be saying that.

Mary: They get every morning now before they go to school and I get them their breakfast. They make their own lunch.

Joe: Oh, yeah, janey! [similar to jeepers]

Mary: Now if they have their lunch ready I can say, then go on upstairs and wash your face and hands and they'll go, that's just automatically every morning. They come down then and get their coats and they're on their way off to school. They would have their breakfast—

Joe: And draw pictures, that's what Emily Evans would be doing—

Mary: Then I'd be at Emily, "Emily!" I'd say. I'd be at Emily about a half an hour—

Joe: [Imitating Emily] "Wait!"

Mary: And at the end I'd say "Emily," and I'd just show her the slipper. And she's over here like a flash. You'd think she was after being killed with the slipper! She goes that fast.

Joe: I don't think I've seen Mary hit Emily with that slipper once.

Mary: I haven't! I just have to show the slipper. She'll come over and she'll get dressed then. I'd say, "Emily, go on up, wash your face and hands. Now, do this."

Joe: [Imitating Emily] "No! Not now! I'm doing this!"

Mary: "Your da is coming downstairs next, the next thing you hear will be your da coming down the stairs." And she'll be off.

Joe: [Imitating Emily, very saccharine] "How're yeh, Daddy!" [Imitating himself] "What're ye doing?" [Imitating Emily] "I'm watching me show." [Imitating himself] "NO! What are ye doing?"

Joe is the final authority in getting Emily to wash her face. He expects his children to respect and respond to his commands. Adapting Beatrice Whiting and Carolyn Edwards's (1988:93–128) discussion of maternal styles to fathering, Joe is neither a "sociable," American-style father nor a "training" parent as we might see in Kenya. Instead, his parental style is a controlling one. Like many parents in more traditional soci-

eties, and like most Irish parents, Joe expects his children to obey him
without question. He understands the father–child relationship to be
one of obedience to authority.

Interestingly, Joe uses some of these understandings while at work,
although this phenomenon is subtle. Joe's FÁS scheme places him as
a school "caretaker," or custodian, from noon until four every weekday.
Joe describes his status as FÁS worker, which does not match the understandings that accompany his status "father." He talks about the
structure of his job, which does not provide an opportunity for the acknowledgment of his expertise and authority:

> It's a very frustrating job. Like, I get paid for four hours and I do
> four hours' work, and if I have to stay a bit later to get the job
> done, I will, even though I don't get paid. For example, there's four
> FÁS workers and a full-time caretaker. The caretaker is, what,
> 67. Now he's the only one with keys; us lowly FÁS workers, we
> don't get keys. Things go walkabout; I can understand the reason-
> ing all right, but it's bleedin' inconvenient sometimes. So maybe
> I'm painting a room and I need white spirits [turpentine] or a
> paintbrush or a rag roller. I have to hunt the fella down, get him
> to stop what he's doing, get him to unlock the shed where the
> things are. He has to stand around and wait for me to get what I
> need, lock it up again, and then go back to what he was doing.
> And if I need something else, if I've forgotten something, it's the
> same routine all over again. It just doesn't make sense, very in-
> efficient. That's not to say anything bad about him, he cares a lot
> about the school. But he's gotten his contract extended now, what,
> three times over the pension age, and he's beginning to get a bit
> past it.

Joe's understanding of himself as an authoritative father is not
matched in his work, where he sees himself treated as a child who
cannot be trusted.

At the same time, Joe sees the other FÁS workers, but not himself,
as in need of something like parental supervision. He considers his
younger colleagues:

> The lads I'm working with, they just don't get how to do a proper
> job. See, the thing is, there's a new fella started about six weeks
> ago. And he just won't do any work, and he won't listen to me, and
> me there for a good while longer. And he's your typical FÁS
> worker, he just won't do anything unless he's pushed to do it. And
> no one will push him. He tries to butter up the people at the school,
> and if they ask him for anything he'll drop whatever he's doing

and do it even if he shouldn't be dropping what he's doing. It's just hard like, because I've worked hard to get things into shape there. And this fella just won't listen to suggestions from me. He's had no training as a painter or builder, no experience, whereas I have. I mean, I know what I'm doing. So, for example. There's this very long corridor outside the principal's office. And, I'll grant him this, it did need painting. But it's an old building, and there's a lot of cracks, especially where there are expanding joists—that's joints that are built to expand with the heat—so there are cracks there where the joints have expanded. And these yokes [things] then need french filling [spackle] before you can paint; otherwise the paint job will be awful and you'll have to do it again in six weeks. And so I told the fella when I saw him setting up that he'd need to do a lot of preparation and did he want some help? No, thanks, he said, I know what I'm doing. Yeah, but it's a big job, I told him. He didn't even respond but set about putting up ladders and getting paint and like that. [Joe then went into a complicated discussion about how to properly treat a wall like this, demonstrating his expertise.] And this lad just started slapping the paint up. And he was using a three-inch brush! No roller, just a small brush! I asked him if he didn't know where the rollers were. I don't know how to use one, he said. He just has to do it in his own way. Though in fairness he did go get a roller. But that doesn't matter, because the wall will need to be redone because he didn't treat it.

Although Joe did not treat his coworker precisely as Joe treats his children, it is clear that Joe feels that his expertise and authority should be recognized by his inferiors—whether they are the less experienced workers or children.[7]

Joe applies behavioral characteristics and expectations associated with the status "father" to work situations. Joe expects to be treated with respect and authority with his children; he expects obedience and acknowledgment of his expertise and greater life experience as a traditional father. Joe carries those expectations with him to work, expecting the "lads," if not the older "fella," to treat him with respect and obedience. Rather than having a strictly separated set of expectations for work and for family life, Joe instead employs aspects of understandings and expectations surrounding "family" statuses in his work life.

Although Joe's role relationships at work and at home are less generalized, in terms of public and private, than are Mary's (see Chapter 6), Joe's experiences show that fathers, as well as mothers, use some understandings and expectations associated with "family," or "private" role relationships in role relationships in work, or conventionally "public," role relationships.

FINBARR O'MALLEY

Finbarr O'Malley has been married to Caroline for twenty years. They have two daughters. Finbarr is in his mid-40s, with a grizzled salt-and-pepper beard and curly gray hair. The O'Malleys live in the middle-class suburb of Clontarf on the north side of Dublin. Finbarr is a teacher and considers himself middle class, having obtained a B.A., an advanced teaching diploma, and an M.A., all through night school. He also considers his brother, a middle-level manager in the civil service, and his sister, a teacher, to be middle class. However, they all came from working-class roots on the north side of Dublin.

Finbarr blends elements of private and public understandings in interesting ways. He discussed Ireland's class structure in terms of education, and always in terms of his own experiences. He spoke with enthusiasm and analysis which clearly stems from his family background; Finbarr seemed to always be teaching, whenever I saw him. So, as Finbarr analyzed the Irish class structure, he used schools as an example:

> In Ireland you can move between the classes much more easily. There are no barriers here—like the schools in England. You have the public and—what do they call the other ones, comprehensives or whatever. Anyway, in England the public schools are fee-paying and in order to get anywhere you have to go to those, but you have to have money to begin with. Here it's not like that. We have very few fee-paying schools; there's not that old boy network like in England. Most of the politicians and the famous people, now, they all went to Christian Brothers schools, and it makes a level playing field, really—no one can get too big for their boots because they've all had the same experience. And it also means that people can move back and forth more easily.

Finbarr knows about schools; he uses his knowledge to understand wider issues. He also tries to use his education at home, to variable effect.

For example, Finbarr noted that he and Caroline had divided household chores based on ability rather than along traditional lines. "I'm no good with wood and like that," he admitted. "Caroline, now, is brilliant with that." He turned to his wife. Caroline picked up the thread of the conversation: "He'll start something and then wander off thinking about something else. Like, we got a VCR and Finbarr started connecting the wires and that. But he got so caught up in the instructions that he began reading them and he left the connection for a long time. I had to wind up doing it—it took me ten minutes to finish something that took him five days!" Finbarr's proclivities toward teaching, instructions, and learning are evident in Caroline's story. He is a teacher and a scholar everywhere. In fact, as Caroline told this story, Finbarr smiled with considerable embarrassment.

However, Finbarr acknowledged that he had few skills that "traditional" fathers should have. If something needs repairing, either Caroline does it, or the item is brought into a shop for repair. Finbarr cannot build shelves or repair electrical wiring as his father could. It did not appear, however, that Finbarr was concerned about that. The only "traditional" understanding Finbarr and Caroline share was that Finbarr should be the breadwinner—and he is. However, that has meant that responsibility for child rearing and housework has fallen almost exclusively on Caroline. She remarked that Finbarr has always worked very hard, with the result that "sometimes I've felt almost like a single parent—he's always had a lot of activities so that most of the parenting fell to me." Finbarr does not do much around the house either. Caroline noted that "I do the cleaning, the cooking, like that. Finbarr loves reading; he'll be holed up after dinner while I do the washing up and like that. But his reading also opens doors for the children; we have books all around now and the girls like to read everything." So Finbarr's occupation, teaching, permeates his family life in complex and interesting ways.

Finbarr consistently shied away from discussing his understandings about child rearing. He referred such questions to Caroline. His daughters frequently teased him affectionately, behaviors he smilingly tolerated most of the time. Caroline was the authority on family matters, not Finbarr. Instead, Finbarr was somewhat removed from the family, willing to discuss political and social issues, usually, as noted above, underscored by education considerations. He seemed to defer to Caroline's expertise regarding the girls, admitting that he had not been all that involved in their upbringing.

Despite Finbarr's relatively distant position in the family, Caroline and he presented a united front.[8] Only now and then would Caroline's occasional resentment of Finbarr's lack of involvement emerge; her discussion of his ineptitude in connecting the VCR was one of the few times Caroline's dissatisfaction showed. No rows, or even hints of arguments brewing, broke out during our times together, unlike the working-class families with whom I worked. It appeared that the particular blend of public and private concerns works well for this family.

Finbarr frequently called upon the understandings underlying his status of "teacher" to shape his behavior in several arenas. He seemed, in the main, to be a teacher at home and at work. He analyzed social issues within the framework of educational concerns. He continually, but subtly, refused to discuss his emotional and family life outside the teacher status. Here, then, with Finbarr, we see a less flexible set of understandings regarding public and private elements. Finbarr seemed to use the same set of understandings in most social situations, whether it be work, family life, or friendship. The analytic distance he established with the status "teacher" crossed social domains. Rather than establishing work and family role relationships based on opposite sets of understandings concerning public and private elements, Finbarr used very similar understandings in different role relationships.

This examination of the lives of Irish fathers shows that most fathers, as well as mothers, use aspects of status understandings and expectations in various social arenas. Rather than employing one set of understandings and expectations while interacting with his family and a different set of understandings and expectations while at work, Irish fathers find parts of the status "father" salient at home *and* at work. In one case, an Irish father seemed to use parts of his status as "teacher" in many different social arenas.

The Irish fathers discussed here demonstrate that the interpenetration of "public" and "private" can be seen in the behavior of Irish fathers with their families and at work. Joe, for example, understands that some of the same behaviors and emotional states appropriate for "traditional" fathers can be applied with his children as with his co-workers. Paul calls upon his status "father" in his business dealings with Omani clients; at the same time, he seems to behave as an irresponsible child, hoping not to be caught out by his boss, the representative of authority. Séamás similarly is affected by his family situation at work; the breakdown of his marriage drastically altered his duties. Séamás found himself revealing private parts of himself to his boss, thus changing the nature of their role relationship and associated understandings. Finbarr was a teacher all the time. In all cases, the domains of public and private are not clearly delineated and are not dichotomous but continuous.

The lives of mothers and fathers in Ireland show that public and private are not separate social arenas. In the next chapter, understandings and experiences of marriage and the marital relationship will be considered. We will see that, for many Irish men and women, the notion that marriage is an emotionally intimate safe haven—the assumption about marriage made by some Western analysts (see Chapter 1)—is not true. Instead, marriage holds different meanings and expectations.

NOTES

1. This is not a strictly Irish phenomenon, of course. The production of children seems the marker of full adulthood in most societies (see, for example, Beidelman 1971; Middleton 1965; or Rogers 1975).

2. Again, this is not necessarily only an Irish pattern. However, this pattern permeates Irish child rearing.

3. "C'mere," an abbreviation of "come here," is a conversation starter and is used to get a listener's attention.

4. The official rate of marital breakdown as shown by census figures, was 6% in 1991 (Ward 1993:7), although most informants said the "real" rate was closer to 25%. Not all separated people admit it to the census bureau or file legal papers for separation. In 1986, 82% of all one-parent households (separated or single parents) were headed by women (Daly 1989:16), suggesting that women overwhelmingly are designated custodial parents either formally or informally.

5. A "bedsit" is a one-room flat in a house converted to rental units; often two or three university students occupy one bedsit to cut costs. Tenants of a bedsit generally have a communal kitchen and bathroom.

6. "Cute," in Irish English, means cleverly manipulative.

7. A few weeks after Joe told this story, the uncooperative coworker came to Joe to ask for help and guidance on how to do the job properly. Joe felt vindicated and was magnanimous in his treatment of the coworker once the coworker had accepted that Joe knew more about construction skills than the coworker did, effectively making Joe the expert.

8. Both Finbarr and Caroline consistently avoided any discussion of their marital relationship, usually by appearing shocked or uncomfortable with questions concerning the relationship, or by "misunderstanding" the question. Information about the emotional quality of their marriage is therefore unavailable. Most middle-class informants refused to discuss their marriage or matters they considered "personal" in any depth. Madsen (personal communication) found this to be true in his research in the United States as well.

CHAPTER 8

Oh, I Couldn't Say That: Intimacy and Marriage in Dublin

Intimacy in Ireland consists of shared experiences much more than shared feelings. Irish and other Western commentators describe Irish marriages as cold, polite, distant, and formal rather than warm and affectionate (Inglis 1987:183–184; Scheper-Hughes 1979:118; Arensberg and Kimball 1968:118). In this chapter, I look at emotional intimacy, especially that experienced in typical Irish marriages, and I examine the influences of the Catholic Church, Ireland's colonial past, and the particular geographic stability of Irish urban life. A marital relationship based on marriage as an institution rather than a relationship remains the norm in Dublin. Although there have been significant changes in Irish allegiances to the Church and Ireland's postcolonial status, the traditional marriage remains important. This shows, among other things, that cultural understandings have remarkable resilience even when religious and political relationships change.

IRISH MARRIAGE

Joe and Mary Evans, described in earlier chapters, have a predominantly traditional Irish marriage. Mary gets the children up in the morning and off to school, while Joe is still asleep. Mary leaves for work before he gets out of bed. Joe goes to work in the early afternoon, before Mary returns, and comes back around tea time. Their evenings consist of the evening meal, watching television, getting the children to bed, and going to bed themselves at different times. Their relationship seems courteous most of the time, although Mary will often overtly criticize Joe for his laziness or for being overweight. She maintains, however, that they get on well. "I love him, I suppose," Mary confides, "but I wouldn't say now I'm in love with him. He's a nice enough fella and all."

Joe, on the other hand, acknowledges that he is desperately and sometimes destructively "mad" for Mary. "I worry all the time that she'll leave me for another fella. I know she doesn't love me like I love her," he says. "So I'll give out to her if she goes to the pub with her friends. It doesn't help though." Joe would not think of telling Mary how insecure and unhappy her distance makes him feel: "Ah, no, now, I couldn't tell her that. I just couldn't. I don't know. It just wouldn't be right."

Mary is aware that Joe is afraid that she will leave him, but she does not often reassure him about her intentions. "Well, that's his problem, really. I wouldn't be going after anyone else; one husband in a lifetime is enough!" Mary laughs. "But it's annoying like." Mary feels that Joe should keep his feelings to himself, as she keeps hers to herself. Any display of emotion is a sign, to Mary, that Joe is a child. Even when fighting, Mary sighs often and rarely raises her voice, while Joe gesticulates and shouts. Mary almost always wins their arguments.

So, for example, one evening just before Christmas I arrived in the middle of a heated argument between Joe and Mary. A long weekend was approaching, and Joe wanted to take the ferry from the Dublin suburb of Dun Laoghaire to Holyhead in Wales. Alcohol is comparatively inexpensive on the boat, since there is a duty-free shop with generous allowances, and Joe and Mary had discussed such a trip rather vaguely a few days before this in my presence. This evening, however, Joe said, "We've been rowing all evening about the fecking trip." Mary sighed. Joe told me, "Well, yer woman there [referring to Mary] doesn't want to go on the boat and we have the days off and all." Mary responded, "Ah now Joe, stop it, will yeh? It's too windy; I'll not go on the boat and anyways it may not sail with the bad weather we're in." She rolled her eyes in frustration. "It'll sail," Joe said with some force as he paced the floor. "You just don't want to go on the boat, but we always have a good time."

"No, Joe," Mary said loudly, "and anyways it's too dear." Joe exaggeratedly pretended amazement. "Too dear, she says," Joe hooted. "It's not too dear. Just ring up the B&I [the steamship company] and you'll find out it's hardly anything at all." Mary sighed heavily. "But why do we need to go on the boat, what's the point?" she asked. Joe looked at Mary in exasperation. "For the booze," he explained with mock patience, heavily ironic. "You know it's cheaper on the boat." He clapped his hands once sharply to punctuate his point and said, "Duty free, yeh see, if all of us go, we'll have a duty-free allowance so I can get cases of beer for very little money."

Mary shook her head vehemently and argued, "But Joe, what do we need all that booze for? Who's going to drink it?" Joe angrily shouted, "You will, and I will, and whoever calls for the Christmas cheer." Mary sighed again and said wearily, "Oh, Joe, no, no, I won't. You know I don't like canned beer." "Ah, sure you do," Joe said with exaggerated deliberation, "and anyway you'd have some lager." Mary raised her voice: "No, I won't! I don't want to go on the boat; it's too dear." Joe insisted even more loudly, "No, it isn't. Here now, I'll prove it to yeh. I'll get the phone book and we'll ring them and find out." "Joe, you can't ring them now, it's too late. No one will be there," Mary sighed another time. Joe looked hard at Mary and said, "Sure I can ring them, just wait, I'll get the phone book. You'll see." Joe left the room.

Mary looked at me, shook her head in disgust, and said, "I don't know why he wants all that beer. We won't drink it."

Joe returned with the Golden Pages, the commercial phone book. He opened it and flipped through it, looking for the steamship line. He found it and pointed out the number to Mary. "Ah, now, Joe, I can't see that," Mary protested. "Yeh can't see that? Where's your glasses?" Joe asked. He turned to me and said, "She can't read a thing without her glasses, but she can't never find them. First sign of old age, yeh know." I pointed to my own glasses and grinned. Joe cleared his throat and said, "Ah, well, sorry." He grinned himself, and the tension level in the room dropped perceptibly. He turned back to Mary. "Let's just call them," he said, and added sarcastically, "dearest. Let's just see how much it is."

Mary refused to give in: "Ah no, Joe, I'd rather go to Belfast anyway." Joe was silent for a minute, clearly considering this. "Belfast? But the train fare for five of us . . ." he mused. "It'd be the same as the boat, or less. They've family fares for the holidays, and the booze'd be cheaper in Belfast just as much as the boat." Joe, defeated, gave in. The family wound up going to Belfast.

This argument followed a typical pattern for Joe and Mary, each told me separately later. Mary hardly raised her voice at all, sighed in a patently obvious way often, and remained in her armchair for the entire row. Joe, on the other hand, shouted frequently, entered and exited the room, gesticulated, and used sarcasm. Although the oldest boy was in the room, they did not involve him in their argument, although each lobbied for my support. As usual, as well, Mary won the argument. She told me on a different occasion that "I gave in to Joe when I agreed to marry him and I won't do it again!" Mary sits firmly but quietly in her disagreements with Joe.

Mary and Joe married because, they say, they had been courting for a year or so, and the "auld wans," in this case the parents, began making plans for them. "Well," Joe says, "really 'twas time to do it. So we took the plunge," in the early 1980s. Mary was in no particular hurry to marry, she said, but Joe was aching to get out of his parents' house, "so I said all right." Once Michael came along, in the mid 1980s, Joe and Mary could relax. "Me da was happy once the grandchildren started," Mary noted. "We could be equals like more or less."

Marriage for Joe and Mary, and for most Irish couples until the last two to three years, is only one step to full Irish adulthood (O'Gorman 1994:103–104). It provides Irish young people with the chance to get out of the house and establish their own home (Humphreys 1966:119), something that otherwise usually is not considered acceptable or economically feasible. Joe and Mary, for instance, both worked full-time before they married and both said that they had saved a significant amount of money in preparation for establishing their own household. It is much more difficult for a single working person to save money if she has to pay for rent, utilities, food, and transportation; so she will usually live with her parents until marriage. In fact, I knew very few unmarried people, other than young university students, who even wanted to live away from the family house. However, until they have children, an Irish couple is not considered completely adult (Scheper-Hughes 1979:136–138). Buying a house, getting married, seeming to deal with life crises with dignity and maturity, obtaining full-time employment or being economically self-sufficient, or holding political or community leadership positions do not constitute full membership in Irish adulthood. It is only the production of children that marks one out as an adult.[1]

However, there are severe restraints on the full expression of oneself within marriage in Ireland. A spouse should be modest, "offering up" physical difficulties and emotional upsets through prayers rather than discussing them. Expressions of emotion and of physical pleasure are generally forbidden in Irish culture, leading to a distant relationship between spouses.

IRISH PHYSICALITY

Some commentators on Irish life (for example, Inglis 1987:184–185; Scheper-Hughes 1979:136–138) associate the prohibition on physical pleasure with what they see as the tyranny of the Catholic Church. Irish sociologist Tom Inglis notes that the Irish Catholic Church dictates that the purpose of sexual intercourse—acceptable only inside marriage—to be procreation; pleasure is at best secondary and often sinful (Inglis 1987:221). He goes on to agree with Scheper-Hughes's assertion (1979:122–125) that the Irish have a specific anxiety about the body and bodily control. This anxiety is molded directly by Church teachings in Ireland, which preach asceticism, physical denial and sacrifice, and suppression of pleasurable physical activities, specifically sex. Therefore, argues Inglis, the Irish, particularly Irish women, come to view sex as an activity that produces children—a desirable result—though the act itself is experienced as distasteful and sinful. One Irishwoman put it this way: "I think there is something wrong with sex and nothing will ever change me . . . One woman friend of mine who is married told me that she felt that after she was married that the loss of her virginity was the greatest loss of her life. And I felt the same way about it . . ." [*sic*] (quoted in Humphreys 1968:139). The distaste for sexual activity and the psychological discomfort attached, remains today among many of my informants, male and female. Informants told me two jokes that express this discomfort. One joke told to me by five different women was, "Why did God create orgasms for women? To give them something else to moan about!" Women told me that this alludes to their constant complaints about their husbands. Another joke, told to me by both men and women, was, "What's the Irish version of foreplay? 'Brace yourself, Brigid!' " Female informants guffawed heartily while telling it and usually added, "That's so true. Just as well." Sex, then, is expected to be, and experienced as, an unpleasant activity. Moreover, one should not discuss sex, either with distaste or with joy, with one's partner, just as other physical pleasures are not discussed.[2]

A general distaste and anxiety surround the revelation of the experience of physical sensations—including emotional–physical reactions—among most Irish people. An Irish person is not supposed to comment on how food tastes, for example; he should "just get it down" instead. Extended discussion of recipes, the taste of food, or even the quantity of food is all taboo, punished through hostile stares, frowning, silence, and overt dismissal of the comment. Instead, the Irish person should be grateful for what appears and eat extremely quickly, apparently ignoring the pleasurable aspects of eating. Furthermore, when an Irish person is ill, he should not describe his physical symptoms. "I have the flu" covers respiratory, stomach, and gastrointestinal complaints. If details of symptoms are offered, sometimes even to doctors, disapproval—through the clear expression of disgust and disinterest—follows quickly. In drinking behavior, the typical Irish man—and some women—gulps down the stout, rather than sipping it with appreciation. Here, too, the Irish person is meant to "get it down" very quickly, often drinking a pint of stout in three swallows. Only here is a hearty appreciative belch allowed; one should not belch or pass gas in the company of others in any other social situation. Finally, an Irish person is not permitted to express any strong emotion. Joe's gesticulations, described above, are discounted by Mary as excessive. The proper Irish person is modest, "offering up" suffering and shunning experience of pleasure. The Church has fostered this Jansenist, ascetic set of cultural understandings. The Irish person should be able to transcend his body, not celebrate it.

IRISH EMOTIONAL UNDERSTANDINGS

Along with Irish physical asceticism is an emotional asceticism. The Church actively discourages the expression of emotional pleasure or upset. Inglis associates this with the Church's interest in appropriating the "civilising" process from the English in the nineteenth century, when the Church took over the education of all Irish children from the British. Inglis comments: "Restraint of the emotions and disciplined behaviour, which were a major characteristic of the civilising process, have always been a major characteristic of the ecclesiastical institutions" (Inglis 1987:134). Because the Church was trying to show the British that it could civilize the undisciplined, rebellious Irish, Inglis argues, it actively worked to squelch any passion or outburst of its members. This can be associated with a general Irish tendency to suppress emotional expression of any kind, and this remains in force today.[3]

Informants confirm the pattern of emotional suppression. One older Limerick woman told me, during a group interview,[4] that this pattern is "the Irish trait. We're the strong and silent type. It's all over our literature, you see it in the short stories. We're meant to bear our problems and say nothing to no one." Her friend agreed but added eagerly, "Yeh, though there always used to be someone you could talk to, an old lady down the road. There'd always be someone you could confide in, who wouldn't spread your business around. It would usually be an old lady of some kind, an older widder woman, she'd be your confidante." The "strong and silent" Irish person could have a sounding board, then, of some kind. But another woman offered more details about the "confidante": "Even with the widder woman, yeh wouldn't have the outward support so much. We show our support through silence really. The support was in the silence. You'd talk but you'd get no words back really. But you knew someone was listening." A fourth woman agreed and continued the discussion by noting that there were things that were "kept in the family." Another woman supported this by telling a story about her own family:

Yeh, that happened in our family. One of my cousins got pregnant when she was a teenager, and her ma and da refused to talk to her. They wouldn't even acknowledge that she was pregnant. They turned her out of the house, so she was on her own. Me aunt, she took her in, got her through the pregnancy. Me cousin then was allowed to go home but she couldn't bring the baby too. So me aunt fostered him. What an awful beginning! What a horror, his mother couldn't even claim him! So much of what the Irish are about is pride, we're keeping it within the family like. It's changing some now; it used to be that we'd never speak about anything.

This woman's story shows that, indeed, the Irish tend to "keep it in." A family secret, understood as shameful by the cousin's parents (but not the aunt), remained a secret until the present day. "His mother couldn't even claim him!" means that the boy does not know that the aunt is not his natural mother. The secrecy surrounding the teenage pregnancy, the disowning of the pregnant girl, and the disavowal of the girl's baby were never discussed by the family, according to this woman. Emotions and family secrets are not supposed to be discussed.

Another woman in this group, in her thirties, picked up on that thought as she discussed Irish emotional patterns. She wistfully remarked that "We're not like that American show, what was it? *The Waltons*? Yeah, that 'good night, John-boy,' 'I love you, Daddy.' Yeah, it would have been nice to have that, to have someone say if you did something good in school. But parents, they'd give no notice, they'd never want to talk about anything." Rather than easy affection freely offered—which seems to be how *The Waltons* were understood by this woman—praise and conversation were only grudgingly given by parents. This group of women was aware that the Irish family patterns in which they were reared tended to squelch what they called "communication" about anything at all.

Another area of secrecy that these women commented on was sex. One woman provoked raucous laughter as she told this story: "Like in our home, if the telly'd be on and they'd be talking about sex at all, me mam would go into the kitchen and start banging pots and pan and the kettle all about so that we couldn't hear what was being heard. No, really, she'd do that, make all that noise so that we wouldn't even hear the word. No one ever talked about sex." Most of the women seemed to find this woman's mother's behavior extreme, but they agreed that it pointed up the inability of Irish parents to talk to their children about anything serious.

Not all women thought that the lack of conversation was entirely harmful. After the woman whose cousin became pregnant wistfully remarked that her parents never talked about anything with her, another woman responded to the disparaging of the "silent way":

> Yeah, though, that silent way wasn't always cold. You'd still communicate like, through the silence. You'd know what the silence meant, you'd get some comfort from it. There was a security in it, a support; you'd just sense it. Like me, I come from ten, I'm the eldest. I always had to help with the younger ones. And me mam, she was always so busy with so many, but she was always aware of what was going on, and we knew she loved us even though she didn't say it. She really knew what was bothering us. She may not have always sat down and talked with us, but there was a comfort in helping her with the chores. It never bothered us. We always felt cared for.

Although this woman was raised in the usual Irish family emotional pattern, she feels well-adjusted and she believes that she was nurtured well. The pattern of emotional suppression, while clearly a part of Irish cultural understandings about privacy, about what can and cannot be said, can produce emotionally healthy adults, as this group of women demonstrates.

However, not all evidence necessarily shows this. It should be remembered that even now the Irish tend to live in small communities, even in large cities. One's behavior is known to those with whom one interacts on a daily basis; social circles are small. The revelation of emotions, then, can be a dangerous business in Irish culture. One of Nancy Scheper-Hughes's informants put it well: " 'To my own ideas, it does great harm, great harm, indeed, to become too intimate with a person. When people become too intimate, they have too much knowledge of each other, and that is very detrimental. You confide in them, and they "soft" it out, and "soft" it out, and you say this and that, and later on you live to regret it' " (Scheper-Hughes 1979:118). Confiding in others is detrimental, because others may use your confidences later on to keep you down. In addition, as one informant remarked, "You wouldn't want to talk about your troubles; it might remind your friend of her own," making your friend feel bad. The acknowledgment of strong emotion, or of problems or triumphs, marks an Irish person out as different from the confidante. This leads to envy, discomfort, and disapproval.

It is widely admitted by the Irish that they have a peculiar habit: begrudgery (Lee 1989:646–648; Clare 1993:7). As discussed in general ways in Chapter 3, begrudgery is the envying of others, dealt with by teasing ("slagging"), mocking, joking, or insulting the person who is envied. If a person has done well in examinations, for example, thereby showing her difference from her schoolmates, it is likely that she will be envied. Recall the young man mentioned in Chapter 3. He tried to set up a business in his small town but was stymied by friends and family: "Me mammy said, 'I love yeh, son, but you're getting too big for your boots.' She thought that if I tried something new I'd likely fail so it would be better to not try." As noted in Chapter 2, he went on to discuss what he called "the lowest common denominator culture" of Ireland. No one should be too good, because that makes other people feel bad about their own inadequacies; if someone is performing poorly, no one should mention it so that he does not feel bad. Scheper-Hughes noticed this in 1970s Kerry, particularly with regard to slagging: "Supposedly good-humored ridicule . . . is used to censure those young men who try to 'shake off village apathy' by trying to get ahead or who demonstrate feelings for others" (Scheper-Hughes 1979:184). In Ireland, whether in the city or "down the country," a person should not mark himself out in any way, through revealing emotions, good news, or new ideas.

There are other, more positive aspect of nonrevelation as well. As we have seen in the discussion of the Limerick women, some Irish people experience silence and lack of discussion of emotional issues as supportive and comforting. Also, most Irish people live in small communities, whether in rural or urban areas. Typically, an Irish man or woman spends his or her life in one neighborhood, and, very likely, in the same house throughout childhood. Irish people are reared, courted, and married, generally in the same area; they die there as well. Childhood friends usually remain friends in adulthood; siblings socialize with each other's extended families; parents remain important until death. People in one's social circle know, therefore, the details of one's life. Discussion of one's job, or one's spouse, or one's life history, is usually not necessary—these are already known. Gossip about others becomes interesting, and political issues are discussed with frequent enthusiasm. In addition, Ireland is culturally homogenous for the most part. An Irish person seems able to intuit what a friend's reaction to a particular life event might be, as her reaction very likely would be similar. Any explanation would be considered superfluous. It would not heighten intimacy. Indeed, such an explanation would create discomfort and distance. Nondisclosure makes cultural sense in Ireland to some extent.

COLONIALISM, THE CHURCH, AND EMOTIONAL REVELATION

We can connect these patterns of nondisclosure with Ireland's colonial experience as well as with the Church's influence. Indeed, the two are intertwined. As Tom Inglis (1987) argues throughout his analysis, the British awarded the Church the opportunity to "civilize" the wild Irish, primarily through turning over control of the Irish educational system in 1831 (Inglis 1987:156–157). The British challenged the Catholic Church to bring the Irish into line, so that the Irish displayed proper Victorian deportment: sobriety, sexual control, literacy, hard work, modest and refined appearance, emotional control, and self-discipline (Inglis 1987:132–134). Church precepts reflected British understandings of proper, civilized behavior—including the suppression of emotional expression. If the Church was successful in civilizing its members, the British would approve and the Church would have, consequently, more control over Catholics than the British did (Inglis 1987: 147). In general, the Church succeeded in its "civilizing" aims.[5]

The Church's attempted abolishment of traditional Irish funerary patterns demonstrates that the Church's aims coincided with the British government's. Irish folklorist Séan O Súilleabháin described the traditional Irish wake as it was structured prior to Church and government intervention, saying that the wake in Ireland used to be a raucous two- or three-day event, as mourners ate heartily, drank heavily, sang, danced, and played games (O Súilleabháin 1967:159–161). The Church in this ritual was virtually ignored by mourners (O Súilleabháin 1967). Now, however, an Irish wake is a quieter affair, only the first part of the entire death ritual. The wake begins a few hours after someone has died and usually lasts through the night. Informants told me that the body of the dead person remains in her home, displayed in the parlor; if the person died in hospital, the body is returned home in a ritual known as "removal." Scheper-Hughes (1979) describes the wake similarly (Scheper-Hughes 1979:123), as do Taylor (1989b) and O Súilleabháin (1967:13–26). A family member should sit with the body at all times, and other mourners file into the parlor, kneel before the body, and say a decade of the rosary or other prayers. After mourners have viewed the body and prayed over it, they join the other mourners, drinking, telling stories, smoking, and eating. The next morning, a decorous Catholic funeral takes place, and the deceased is immediately buried.

Taylor (Taylor 1989b:182) and O Súilleabháin (1967:146–157) agree with Inglis's contention that the Church was attempting to "tame" the "wild" Irish. Taylor argues that, as the Church tried to gain more control of the lives of its Irish parishioners, it appropriated death and surrounding rituals as the most powerful in the life of a community (Taylor 1989b:182). However, Taylor further remarks that the community did not necessarily agree with the Church's vision of the meaning of death—an opportunity to teach the living about sacrifice and eternal life—and mourners continued their wake practices despite, or perhaps because of, the warnings of the Church (Taylor 1989b). Similarly,

O Súilleabháin discusses official Church records from the 1700s in which it is clear that the Church in Ireland repeatedly has attempted, and repeatedly has failed, to curb Irish wake customs (O Súilleabháin 1967:146–157). The Church's continuing reshaping of traditions and practices surrounding death provide evidence of the Church's interest in "civilizing" the Irish to meet nineteenth-century English standards of deportment and behavior.

In one way, though, the Church did not meet Victorian standards. The notion that there is some value in instrumental, rational, individualized behavior is largely rejected by the Church. The development of an individualized conscience, based on a personal ethical and moral code reached after careful reflection, is not salient to Catholic practice. Inglis argues that "the Church's teaching that salvation is attained by following its rules and regulations has discouraged individuals from making up their own minds about what is right and wrong. This, combined with an emphasis on frugal comfort and a suppression of individual interests in favour of those of Church, family, and community, has been associated with an absence of a rugged, ambitious individualism which is a feature of fully developed societies" (Inglis 1987:72). Inglis is arguing that the Irish Catholic Church emphasizes one's responsibilities to it, first of all, and to others secondly. One's own interests, emotions, experiences, and thoughts are very nearly irrelevant for a proper Catholic, in this view. A person should take no risks and should reveal no vulnerabilities, offering up personal suffering in prayer instead. One cannot have initiative and new ideas. Mary Loughane (1983) as well very briefly argues that the "rugged individualism" model of social relations, particularly evinced by sociologist Talcott Parsons, is only one among many ways to understand the world. Although she agrees that the Catholic Church in Ireland has discouraged independent thought and thus independent action and ambition, she also asserts that this is not necessarily a bad thing. Self-actualization is one way to be psychologically healthy, but, Loughane says, it is a peculiarly Anglo-Protestant way, not necessarily relevant to the Irish Catholic experience (Loughane 1983:8–9).

Begrudgery can be seen as merely a secular enactment of the Catholic Church viewpoint. If one should try to do something new or challenge the established order, whether it be business, family, or religious authority, one is directly opposing the Catholic Church. As shown in Chapter 2, the Church discourages, even now, open questioning of Catholic leaders; yet, as noted in Chapter 2, in general Irish people still attend Mass once a week. It may be that secular and religious cultural understandings regarding the inappropriate nature of challenges to authority, as well as prohibitions on the expression of emotion, fit well, providing little discomfort or dissonance for Irish people. The Church says that little of an emotional nature should be revealed and that its dictates will not be questioned by a good Catholic. Begrudgery requires, similarly, that a person may not challenge the established social order. Display of emotions and overt challenges to authority are culturally forbidden. Catholic practice, attendance at Mass, suppression of emotions, and bedgrudgery, then, make cultural sense. Revelation of emotional dissatisfaction is therefore indeed a dangerous business.

IRISH MARRIAGE AND INTIMACY

These cultural understandings about intimacy and the revelation of emotions obtain in marriage as much as they do in village or neighborhood life. Church disapproval of the expression of emotion, coupled with the Irish prohibition on disclosure, fits well with an emotionally distant marital relationship. Joe therefore is horrified by the thought of revealing his dissatisfaction to Mary. Similarly, Mary would never acknowledge that Joe has deep emotions about her. In part, this is due to Irish discomfort with revelation; in some ways it is also not necessary.

Further, Irish marriage primarily has been based more on understandings of it as an institution rather than as a relationship. Irish family therapist Gabriel Kiely, in a book aimed at Irish psychotherapists, remarks that "institutional marriage" consists of nonrevelation, strict gender role relationships, and bonds based on duty; it is the idea of marriage that is crucial (Kiely 1989:45).[6] Kiely argues that "companionship marriage" is emerging in Irish society. This is a marriage based on emotional sharing, role relationships based on ability and personality rather than solely a sexual division of labor, and bonds based on love; the relationship is valued more than the institution (Kiely 1989: 45). Companionship marriage in Ireland is relatively new, although Irish psychotherapists like Kiely are encouraging this kind of marital relationship; for instance, Irish psychotherapists Paul Andrews (1994) and Tony Humphreys (1994) provide similar exhortations. Few informants seem to have such marriages, however, and they do not seem interested in changing their marriages.

PUBLIC AND PRIVATE IN IRISH INTIMACY

Irish intimacy, marital and otherwise, consists of shared experiences much more than shared feelings. The Parsonian distinction between instrumental and emotionally laden relationships does not seem especially salient to everyday Irish life. The Irish family, and the Irish marriage, is not the private comforting arena that family scholars argue a typical family is (see Chapter 1). Individuals in Irish intimate relationships use a different set of understandings regarding privacy and public life than do social theorists such as Talcott Parsons or Christopher Lasch.

Privacy, for the Irish, is material revealed to absolutely no one, as noted in Chapter 5. The Church's prohibition on emotional and physical indulgence, associated in part with British colonialism, means that emotional expression is culturally discouraged. Not only is one culturally forbidden to reveal emotional vulnerabilities, but an individual Irish Catholic ought to rise above such vulnerabilities, offering her suffering to the glory of God. Instead of discussion of feelings, the Irish establish intimacy through longevity of relationships. Long-term interaction, and even silence, over many years, creates closeness.

This means that a good many interactions will contain cultural understandings that mix aspects of formality and informality, of public and private. A person does not have to, and is forbidden to, discuss his particular life circumstances with friends and, importantly, with family. He can offer, however, new information and facts when, for example, discussing work with his spouse. Such everyday interaction creates further Irish intimacy. Emotions will not be analyzed, though events will be.

Conversely, an Irish person does not discuss her family or the details of her job with friends, much less strangers. We saw in Chapter 6 that neither Jeanne nor Mary would discuss family issues with co-workers except in very general terms. Private understandings are used to structure work relationships to some extent, but those understandings are not those of emotional revelation. Joe used aspects of his understandings regarding his status as father while working with younger men, but he did not discuss that process with them; indeed, he was unaware that he was doing it.

Aspects of the public and of private life work together to create a specifically Irish intimacy. Irish marriages, like all other social relationships, are structured by cultural understandings regarding what is appropriately revealed and what is not. Intimacy in Ireland contains elements quite different from the picture painted by most social scientists discussing private life and public life.

NOTES

1. Infertility and homosexuality generally are seen as "unnatural" states, as is remaining single unless one is called to a religious vocation. Such situations are either pitied, or, in the case of homosexuality, are considered completely immoral and a horrible deviation from the natural order.

2. I suspect that it is remotely possible that Irish people discuss sexual ac-

tivities with their priests. However, people do not seem to go to Confession very much. The Church requires, at the very least, an annual Confession: "each of the faithful is bound by an obligation faithfully to confess serious sins at least once a year" (*Catechism of the Catholic Church* 1994: §1457). I have figures only from 1974 dealing with self-reported attendance at Confession: 98.8% of all respondents said that they went at least three times a year (Phádraig 1976: 116–119). Most of my informants did not fulfill that obligation.

3. Scheper-Hughes's analysis (1979), while similar to Inglis's, is ahistorical. Scheper-Hughes discusses the Irish tendency to "keep it in," whether "it" is emotion or physical sensation, associating that with an Irish anxiety about bodily emissions and corporeality.

4. This group was taking a psychology class. There were about fifteen women in the class.

5. See Inglis (1987) for further discussion of the British effect on marriage patterns; Scheper-Hughes (1979) indirectly discusses this as well. Briefly, the British disapproved of the Irish inheritance system and insisted that the Irish father designate only one heir instead. Irish parents had to choose one son to inherit the family farm, rather than dividing available land among all sons (and occasionally a daughter) as had been the practice before the Famine. This resulted in very late marriages coupled with high rates of fertility, emigration, considerable celibacy, and the infantilization of the inheritor well into late adulthood (Scheper-Hughes 1979). A son had to suppress his sexual desires, as well as his emotions, if he wanted to remain the heir. It could be that this nineteenth-century pattern still has some effect on Irish marriage and emotional life today.

6. Interestingly, Rogers's (1975) description of marriage in rural France is similar. She discusses French peasant marriage as marked by strict gender segregation and a division of labor along gender lines, as well as not revealing one's emotions.

CHAPTER 9

Conclusion: Marriage in Private and Public

IRISH TIES

Using urban working-class family life in Ireland, I have argued that public life and private life should in most cases be understood to be blends of relationships, rather than separate social arenas. Rather than a dichotomy, we can see an interaction or series of interactions between participants in role relationships as containing more or less public or private elements, identification of which can help characterize the interaction(s) more precisely. There is some behavior that is almost entirely private; there is some that is nearly completely public; and most behavior falls somewhere between the two.

Private life was defined here as consisting of relationships that are more or less ongoing, continual, and characterized by general reciprocity and multiplexity. First, these relationships are usually marked by limited access: partners in such relationships have access to information that those outside the relationship do not have. Second, private relationships often contain mutual disclosure of information (though not necessarily the exchange of emotional vulnerabilities), which varies cross-culturally. Third, the relationships are generally culturally recognized as valuable and inviolable. Fourth, expectations of partners in private relationships are frequently flexible and generalized rather than concrete and limited. If a relationship does not contain these elements, it is more than likely not private.

However, in everyday life, aspects of private relationships cross what has been seen conventionally as the public/private boundary. As was seen through analysis of the behavior of Irish mothers and fathers, as well as through a more general discussion of Irish social life, aspects of private relationships are used by individuals in interactions outside those relationships. So, for example, Joe Evans uses aspects of fatherhood in his working life. His work and his family are not dichotomous experiences for him. Joe's wife, Mary, also finds ways to use her understandings of motherhood in her work, again showing that public life and private life are not discontinuous social arenas.

Many scholars have employed a rigid dichotomy to characterize public life and private life, in contravention of everyday social experience; I examined some of these. I argued that these studies were defective in that scholars continue to use the conventional dichotomy of public and private, despite their claims to the contrary. Similarities were seen in a discussion of ethnographies of everyday experience at work. I discussed Ireland's colonial past and provided a brief overview of Irish society, Dublin's history and current organization, as well as previous ethnography of Ireland and a few observations on modern Irish culture. We saw how the framework of elements of public and private understandings works in Dublin relationships, in motherhood, and in fatherhood.

Finally, I looked at how Ireland's colonial past and the still strong influence of the Catholic Church have shaped Irish understandings regarding proper emotional expression and experience. In that chapter, I concluded that Irish Catholic ideology, as well as the face-to-face nature of Irish life even in urban areas, has encouraged the Irish to deny physical pleasure and overt, florid emotional expression. This in turn can be correlated with a specifically Irish understanding of private, intimate life, which consists of shared experiences rather than openly shared emotions. However, as Ireland faces the twenty-first century, it appears that new sets of understandings are being encouraged, as we saw from recent survey results. Perhaps private life is not the only affective realm in which we participate, either in Ireland or in a good part of the world.

INSTITUTIONAL MARRIAGE AND COMPANIONATE MARRIAGE

As we saw in Chapter 8, Irish psychotherapists are urging Irish couples toward an American-style marriage relationship and away from more traditional marital interaction. More generally, we can follow William Goode (1970) and differentiate between institutional and companionate or conjugal marriages. That is, an institutional or traditional marriage is one based on clearly defined tasks allocated by gender rather than ability; it includes strong cultural understandings surrounding duty and obligation as well as rights. In traditional marriages, women are subservient to men, and younger people to older. The institutional marriage is task-oriented, both economically and regarding child rearing (in that women take the primary responsibility for nurtuance while men eventually train their sons—and only their sons, not their daughters—in "public" responsibilities); spouses in such a marriage do not expect that substantial emotional sharing and mutual psychosocial intimacy will provide a fundamental basis for the marriage. Friends and relatives other than spouses provide that intimacy. I have argued throughout that many Irish marriages fit the institutional pattern.

In contrast, the conjugal or companionate marriage serves as the American dominant cultural ideal—that is, white middle-class expectations shape this ideal. Certainly the model seems to be spreading to many places beyond the United States, but Americans seem to have made the companionate marriage an art form (I base these conclusions in large part on my experience as a family therapist, an anthropologist at home and abroad, and as an active participant in American heterosexual culture). In these marriages, spouses expect sharing of all kinds. Men and women are to discuss their emotions in depth; they are to reveal vulnerabilities openly to their spouses; they are to participate equally in household and child-rearing chores; there is to be an ethos of equality and deep and exclusive friendship as the foundation of the marital relationship. Couples are expected to find time for themselves as a couple; the relationship is marked off as separate from the family and is just as, if not more, valuable, than the more child-centered aspects of family life. Choice organizes many of these marriages: partners in conjugal marriages are chosen freely, and in general they can be discarded almost as easily too if the emotional quality of the relationship seriously deteriorates. Some Irish marriages strain toward elements of the conjugal marriage, but on the whole the Irish retain traditional marital patterns. I suspect, however, that, given the rapid pace of societal and cultural change in Ireland, marital relationships are, and will continue to be, changing quickly.

There has been some scholarly work examining the nature of marital relationships and investigating how, or whether, emotional intimacy is indeed a basic and necessary component for marriages universally. In large part, these are by necessity comparative or anthropological works; it seems to me that most Western, and especially American, psychological and psychotherapeutic work assumes, without empirical verification, that the companionate marriage is the most healthy and functional style around. What seems clear, even from the brief discussion above, is that it is not. Even in the United States, the most aggressive promoter of egalitarian, companionate marriage, working-class marriages seem less likely to conform to the model. And it appears questionable that the middle class can meet its own ideal (Hochschild 1997); indeed, Naomi Quinn's (1996) exploration of middle-class understandings of marriage bears this out. Finally—and Goode pointed this out thirty years ago—a marriage based solely on choice, emotion, and "love" is a very weak one indeed (when feelings—the basis of the marriage—change, there are few options but to end the relationship).

Xiaohe Xu demonstrates this in a comparative study of marriage in modern urban China and America (1998). Not surprisingly, American marriages seem firmly grounded in the promises and problems of companionate marriage (Xiaohe 1998:124–125). What may be more interesting is that Chinese marriages, long held to be institutional marriages, also seem to be adopting some companionate elements. Goode predicted that a companionate marriage, unstable as it is, would result in both more gender equality and more marriage breakdown, and, in China as in the United States, this seems to be the case (Xiaohe 1998). One conclusion that we can draw, then, is that with the adoption of companionate marital relationships—that is, with the adoption of marriage as a strictly private relationship—marital instability is a frequent result. Certainly in Ireland the increasing number of legal separations finally forced the divorce issue, and it is likely that at least some of these separations were due to an increasingly intolerable distance in what the Irish have begun to believe is supposed to be an emotionally and physically intimate connection.

What Americans rarely acknowledge, at least conventionally, is that a companionate, privatized marriage is an incredibly difficult relationship to sustain over an increasingly long period of time. Our freedom of choice, our sentimentalization of eternal love, our expectations (usually dashed) for emotional and sexual fidelity, and our belief that marriage belongs only to the direct participants—the spouses (why else are there so many in-law jokes?)—are really quite unrealistic. Barbara Ehrenreich, the noted American social commentator, remarks that we expect far too much out of marriage: "What we lack is not [family] 'values' but the old-fashioned neighborhood or community. Once, people found companionship among their old high-school buddies, and got help with child raising from granddads and aunts. Marriages lasted because less was expected of them. If you wanted a bridge partner or a plumber or a confidant, you had a whole village to choose from. Today we don't marry a person—i.e., an actual human being, with all the attendant failings and limits—we attempt to marry a village" [*sic*] (Ehrenreich 1995:15). Moreover, "expert" comments following the Kenneth Starr allegations regarding President Bill Clinton's sexual behavior only encourage an unrealistic marital relationship. For instance, New York psychologist Don-David Lusterman was reported to have advised, at the height of the Clinton scandal, that spouses should not discuss their emotions with anyone but each other: "Even platonic intimacies, such as discussing personal matters at lunch or over e-mail [with colleagues], make you vulnerable [to infidelity]" (Barry 1998: 7L). Lusterman seems to be advising American spouses to invest all significant emotional energy in one other person—the spouse—rather than recognizing that one person cannot fill all needs for another. What this means is that the characteristics of a companionate marriage—actually not too terrible a set of understandings, within bounds, for a relationship—become, in typical American style, overdone, exaggerated, and imbued with an unreasonably rigid morality that this kind of marriage simply cannot support.

To understand the actuality of marriage and private life in general more fully, we need to continue the scholarly work that has been started. Xiaohe Xu's (1998) study, discussed above, is a good example of how to get at the essence of marriage as we face the twenty-first century. Stanley Kurtz's (1992) survey of Hindu marriage and family life, in which he demonstrates the danger of a private marriage for the functioning of an extended family, also provides some hints for understanding marriage on the ground, as does Steve Derné's (1992) discussion of Hindu men's experience of self in family context. Gary Robinson's (1997) analysis of Tiwi understandings of gender, hierarchy, and loyalty shows that, at least for first marriages, Tiwi men and women prefer institutional marriage for practical, extended-family reasons. Katherine Ewing (1991) looks at the experiences of in-marrying Pakistani women, showing that of all the new relationships established following a marriage, the bride must concentrate much harder on her new in-laws and neighbors rather than her husband; she does not seek the groom's companionship in the way she might in a conjugal marriage for very good psychosocial reasons.

The idea that one person can fill all emotional, sexual, physical, intellectual, and moral needs of another provides a marriage ideal doomed to failure, it seems. This is especially true for Americans, who keep adding years to the life span and, not surprisingly, divorce at ever-increasing rates. It could well be that we did not evolve as monogamous pair-bonders as evolutionary psychologists assert (Wright 1996); we simply died, or were killed, before the idea of a new partner occurred to us. An institutional marriage seems far better suited to a longer life span than does a companionate marriage—or, perhaps, some reasonable mixture of the two. And, in fact, marriages that do last through the life span probably blend the highly privatized, love-based companionate marriage with more traditional elements (surely more research is called for there). But steadfastly pushing marriage into a realm of the private for which the institution was never designed may kill marriage off yet.

I should note that I most certainly am *not* advocating an American return to overtly family-arranged unions aimed at enhancing extended-family finances and prestige. Even a cursory glance at patrilineal and, less often, matrilineal marriage arrangements shows that these kinds of marriages encourage patriarchal influence, without doubt oppressing women to an onerous degree far beyond conjugal marriages (which are, of course, too oppressive as they exist now). That surely is a poor solution to this conundrum. However, the American version of companionate marriage clearly is not working either. A return to "family values" will not work, as it oppresses women and places far too many expectations on an originally structurally unsound relationship. I suggest that a marriage with goals of less exclusivity may work, as exclusiveness does seem unnatural (Small 1995); given the increasing reliability of contraceptive technology, it may be that we need finally to lose the notion that sexual or emotional exclusivity is possible for a good part of the population. At the least, we need to recognize that to reduce our emotional connection to one person for upwards of fifty years is psychologically and biologically unhealthy. Other societies seem to show us this.

Finally, then, marriage as the ultimate, exclusive, intimate, emotionally laden, private relationship does not, as a general practice, seem either to work very well or to exist in a pure form in too many places. Rather than calls for a return to a narrowly defined "family values," it may behoove us to understand how marriage works as a human— rather than just American—institution. Perhaps this investigation into a society many Americans claim as their own—Ireland—helps demonstrate the danger of assuming the universality of what are clearly American experiences of public and private life.

References

Anderson, Lisa. 1995. "Divorce, Irish Style." *Chicago Tribune*, December 3, 1995. Section 2. Pp. 1, 10.

Andrews, Paul. 1994. *Changing Children: Living with a New Generation*. Dublin: Gill and Macmillan.

Ardagh, John. 1994. *Ireland and the Irish: Portrait of a Changing Society*. London: Hamish Hamilton.

Arensberg, Conrad. 1937. *The Irish Countryman*. New York: American Museum Science Books.

Arensberg, Conrad, and Solon Kimball. 1968. *Family and Community in Ireland*. Gloucester, MA: Peter Smith.

Barry, John. 1998. "Infidelity May Be More Subtle than a 1-Night Stand." *Milwaukee Journal-Sentinel*, August 30, 1998. Pp. 1L, 7L.

Beale, Jenny. 1986. *Women in Ireland: Voices of Change*. Dublin: Gill and Macmillan.

Beidelman, T. O. 1971. *The Kaguru: A Matrilineal People of East Africa*. Prospect Heights, IL: The Waveland Press.

Bellah, Robert N., Richard Madsen, William M. Sullivan, Ann Swidler, and Steven M. Tipton. 1985. *Habits of the Heart: Individualism and Commitment in American Life*. New York: Harper and Row.

Bensman, Joseph, and Robert Lilienfeld. 1979. *Between Public and Private: The Lost Boundaries of the Self*. New York: Free Press.

Bott, Elizabeth. 1971 [1957]. *Family and Social Network: Roles, Norms, and External Relationships in Ordinary Urban Families*. 2d ed. London: Tavistock Publications.

Brain, Robert. 1976. *Friends and Lovers*. New York: Basic Books.

Breen, Richard, Damian F. Hannan, David P. Rottman, and Christopher T. Whelan. 1990. *Understanding Contemporary Ireland: State, Class and Development in the Republic of Ireland*. Dublin: Gill & Macmillan.

Brody, Hugh. 1973. *Inishkillane: Change and Decline in the West of Ireland*. London: Allen Lane.

Brown, Terrence. 1985. *Ireland: A Social and Cultural History, 1922–1985*. London: Fontana Press.

Browne, Noël. 1986. *Against the Tide*. Dublin: Gill and Macmillan.

Cahill, Thomas. 1995. *How the Irish Saved Civilization: The Untold Story of Ireland's Heroic Role from the Fall of Rome to the Rise of Medieval Europe*. New York: Anchor Books Doubleday.

Catechism of the Catholic Church. 1994. Chicago: Loyola University Press.

Clare, Anthony. 1993. "The mad Irish?" In *Mental Health in Ireland*. Colm Keane, ed. Pp. 4–17. Dublin: Gill and Macmillan.

Clayre, Alasdair. 1974. *Work and Play: Ideas and Experience of Work and Leisure*. London: Weidenfeld and Nicolson.

Clifford, James. 1986. "Introduction: Partial Truths." In *Writing Culture: The Poetics and Politics of Ethnography*. James Clifford and George E. Marcus, eds. Pp. 1–26. Berkeley and Los Angeles: University of California Press.

Collier, Jane, and Sylvia Yanagisako. 1988. "Toward a Unified Analysis of Gender and Kinship." In *Gender and Kinship: Essays Toward a Unified Analysis*. Jane Collier and Sylvia Yanagisako, eds. Pp. 14–50. Stanford, CA: Stanford University Press.

Constitution of Ireland. 1990 [1937]. Dublin: Government Publications.

———. 1998. Electronic document. http://www.maths.tcd.ie/pub/Constitution/Articles40–44.html.

Coontz, Stephanie. 1988. *The Social Origins of Private Life: A History of American Families, 1600–1900*. London: Verso.

———. 1992. *The Way We Never Were: American Families and the Nostalgia Trap*. New York: Basic Books.

Corish, Patrick. 1985. *The Irish Catholic Experience: A Historical Survey*. Dublin: Gill and Macmillan.

Crotty, Raymond. 1993. "A System That Cannot Deliver." In *The Jobs Crisis*. Colm Keane, ed. Pp. 64–74. Dublin: Mercier Press.

Cullen, Sandra. 1994. "Culture, Gender, and Organizational Change in British Welfare Benefits Services." In *Anthropology of Organizations*. Susan Wright, ed. Pp. 140–157. London: Routledge.

Curry, John. 1993. *Irish Social Services*. 2d ed. Dublin: Institute of Public Administration.

Curtin, Chris, Hastings Donnan, and Thomas M. Wilson, eds. 1994. "Anthropology and Irish Urban Settings." In *Irish Urban Cultures*. Chris Curtin, Hastings Donnan, and Thomas M. Wilson, eds. Pp. 1–21. Belfast: Queen's University of Belfast [Institute of Irish Studies].

Curtin, Chris, Pauline Jackson, and Barbara O'Connor, eds. 1987. *Gender in Irish Society*. Galway: Galway University Press.

Curtin, Chris, Mary Kelly, and Liam O'Dowd, eds. 1984. *Culture and Ideology in Ireland*. Galway: Galway University Press.

Daly, Mary. 1989. *Women and Poverty*. Dublin: Attic Press.

Derné, Steve. 1992. "Beyond Institutional and Impulsive Conceptions of Self: Family Structure and the Socially Anchored Self." *Ethos* 20:259–288.

Dillon, Michelle. 1993. *Debating Divorce: Moral Conflict in Ireland*. Lexington: University Press of Kentucky.

Dudley, Kathryn. 1994. *The End of the Line: Lost Jobs, New Lives in Postindustrial America*. Chicago: University of Chicago Press.

Durkheim, Emile. 1961. "On Mechanical and Organic Solidarity." In *Theories of Society: Foundations of Modern Sociology*. Talcott Parsons, Edward Shils, Kaspar D. Naegele, and Jesse R. Pitts, eds. Pp. 208–213. Glencoe, IL: Free Press.

Ehrenreich, Barbara. 1995. *The Snarling Citizen: Essays*. New York: Harper-Perennial.

European Communities Encyclopedia and Directory. 1992. London: Europa Publishing.

Evans-Pritchard, E. E. 1940. *The Nuer: A Description of the Modes of Livelihood and Political Institutions of a Nilotic People*. New York: Oxford University Press.

———. 1951. *Kinship and Marriage Among the Nuer*. Oxford: Oxford University Press.

Ewing, Katherine P. 1991. "Can Psychoanalytic Theories Explain the Pakistani Woman? Intrapsychic Autonomy and Interpersonal Engagement in the Extended Family." *Ethos* 19:131–160.

Family Matters. February 9, 1994. Radio Telefis Éireann 1, Dublin.

Fanon, Frantz. 1967. *Black Skin, White Masks*. New York: Grove Press.

———. 1968. *The Wretched of the Earth*. New York: Grove Press.

Ferree, Myra Marx. 1984. "Sacrifice, Satisfaction, and Social Change: Employment and the Family." In *My Troubles Are Going to Have Trouble With Me: Everyday Trials and Triumphs of Women Workers*. Karen B. Sacks and Dorothy Remy, eds. Pp. 61–79. New Brunswick, NJ: Rutgers University Press.

Fortes, Meyer. 1969. *Kinship and the Social Order: The Legacy of Lewis Henry Morgan*. Chicago: Aldine Publishing Company.

Fox, Robin. 1978. *The Tory Islanders: A People of the Celtic Fringe*. Cambridge: Cambridge University Press.

———. 1983 [1967]. *Kinship and Marriage: An Anthropological Perspective*. Cambridge: Cambridge University Press.

Furstenberg, Frank. 1996. "The Future of Marriage." *American Demographics* 18:34–40.

Gaffin, Dennis. 1995. "The Production of Emotion and Social Control: Taunting, Anger, and the Rukka in the Faeroe Islands." *Ethos* 23:149–172.

Gerstel, Naomi, and Harriet Engel Gross. 1987. Introduction and overview. In *Families and Work*. Naomi Gerstel and Harriet Engel Gross, eds. Pp. 1–21. Philadephia, PA: Temple University Press.

Goode, William J. 1970. *World Revolution and Family Patterns*. New York: Free Press.

Graham, B. J. 1993. "Early Medieval Ireland: Settlement as an Indicator of Economic and Social Transformation, c. 500–1100." In *An Historical Geography of Ireland*. B. J. Graham and L. J. Proudfoot, eds. Pp. 19–57. London: Academic Press.

Gwynn, Stephen. 1938. *Dublin Old and New*. London: Geo. G. Harrap.

Haley, Jay. 1980. *Leaving Home: The Therapy of Disturbed Young People*. New York: McGraw-Hill.

Hardiman, Niamh, and Christopher T. Whelan. 1994. "Politics and Democratic Values." In *Values and Social Change in Ireland*. Christopher T. Whelan, ed. Pp. 100–135. Dublin: Gill and Macmillan.

Harris, Marvin. 1979. *Cultural Materialism: The Struggle for a Science of Culture*. New York: Random House.

Haughey, Nuala. 1997a. "Church May Face £1.5m Claims over Smyth." *Irish Times*, July 26. Electronic document. http://www.irish-times.com/irish%2Dtimes/paper/1997/0726/fro2.html.

———. 1997b. "Pied Piper Figure Spread Stain of Sin for 35 Years." *Irish Times*, August 23. Electronic document. http://www.irish-times.com/irish%2Dtimes/paper/1997/0823/hom1.html.

Hite, Shere. June 4, 1995. "Interview." *Weekend Edition–Sunday*. National Public Radio. KPBS, San Diego.

Hochschild, Arlie. 1983. *The Managed Heart: Commercialization of Human Feeling*. Berkeley: University of California Press.

———. 1989. *The Second Shift*. New York: Avon.

———. 1997. *The Time Bind: When Work Becomes Home & Home Becomes Work*. New York: Metropolitan Books.

Hornsby-Smith, Michael P., and Christopher T. Whelan. 1994. "Religious and Moral Values." In *Values and Social Change in Ireland*. Christopher T. Whelan, ed. Pp. 7–44. Dublin: Gill and Macmillan.

Humphreys, Alexander. 1966. *New Dubliners: Urbanization and the Irish Family*. New York: Fordham University Press.

Humphreys, Tony. 1994. *The Family: Love It and Leave It*. Cork: Carraig Print.

Inglis, Tom. 1987. *Moral Monopoly: The Catholic Church in Modern Irish Society*. Dublin: Gill and Macmillan.

Institute for Public Administration. 1994. *Administrative Yearbook and Diary, 1994*. Dublin: Institute for Public Administration.

Jameson, Frederick. 1984. "Postmodernism, or the Cultural Logic of Late Capitalism." *New Left Review* 146:53–92.

John Paul II. 1982. *On the Family: Apostolic Exhortation (Familiaris Consortio)*. Washington, DC: United States Catholic Conference.

Johnson, Paul. 1980. *Ireland: A Concise History from the Twelfth Century to the Present Day*. Chicago: Academy Chicago Publishers.

Kane, Eileen. 1977. *The Last Place God Made: Traditional Economy and New Industry in Rural Ireland*. 4 vols. New Haven: Human Relations Area Files.

———. 1979. "The Changing Role of the Family in a Rural Irish Community." *Journal of Comparative Family Studies* 10:141–162.

Kanter, Rosabeth Ross. 1977. *Men and Women of the Corporation*. New York: Basic Books.

Kiely, Gabriel. 1989. *Finding Love: Counselling for Couples in Crisis*. Dublin: Poolbeg.

Klatch, Rebecca. 1987. *Women of the New Right*. Philadelphia, PA: Temple University Press.

Komito, Lee. 1985. "Politics and Clientelism in Urban Ireland: Information, Reputation, and Brokerage." Ann Arbor, MI: University Microfilms.

———. 1989. "Dublin Politics: Symbolic Dimensions of Clientelism." In *Ireland from Below: Social Change and Local Communities*. Chris Curtin and Thomas M. Wilson, eds. Pp. 240–259. Galway: Galway University Press.

———. 1994. "Personalism and Brokerage in Dublin Politics." In *Irish Urban Cultures*. Chris Curtin, Hastings Donnan, and Thomas M. Wilson, eds. Pp. 79–98. Belfast: Queen's University of Belfast [Institute of Irish Studies].

Kuhn, Thomas. 1962. *The Structure of Scientific Revolutions*. Chicago: University of Chicago Press.

Kurtz, Stanley N. 1992. *All the Mothers Are One: Hindu India and the Cultural Reshaping of Psychoanalysis*. New York: Columbia University Press.

Lasch, Christopher. 1977. *Haven in a Heartless World: The Family Besieged*. New York: Basic Books.

Laslett, Peter. 1977. *Family Life and Illicit Love in Earlier Generations: Essays in Historical Sociology*. Cambridge: Cambridge University Press.

Laufer, Robert S., and Maxine Wolf. 1977. "Privacy as a Concept and a Social Issue: A Multidimensional Developmental Theory." *Journal of Social Issues* 33:22–42.

Lee, J. J. 1989. *Ireland 1912–1985: Politics and Society*. Cambridge: Cambridge University Press.

Loughane, Mary Fionula. 1983. "Through Irish Eyes: A Mainly Women's Perspective on the Influence of Women and Men in Irish Families." Ann Arbor, MI: University Microfilms International.

McCafferty, Nell. 1987. *Goodnight Sisters . . .* Dublin: Attic Press.

McGarry, Patsy. 1997. "Time to Invite Bishop Casey to Return Home." *Irish Times*, December 8. Electronic document. http://www.irish-times.com/irish%2Dtimes/paper/1997/1208/opt5.html.

MacSiomóin, Tomás. 1994. "The Colonised mind—Irish Language and Society." In *Reconsiderations of Irish History and Culture: Selected Papers from the Desmond Greaves Summer School, 1989–93*. Daltún Ó Ceallaigh, ed. Pp. 27– 41. Dublin: Léirmheas.

Madanes, Cloé. 1981. *Strategic Family Therapy*. San Francisco: Jossey-Bass.

Margulis, Stephen T. 1977. "Conceptions of Privacy: Current Status and Next Steps." *Journal of Social Issues* 33:5–19.

Medick, Hans, and David Warren Sabean. 1984. "Interest and Emotion in Family and Kinship Studies." In *Interest and Emotion: Essays on the Study of Family and Kinship*. Hans Medick and David Warren Sabean, eds. Pp. 9–27. Cambridge: Cambridge University Press.

Memmi, Albert. 1965. *The Colonizer and the Colonized*. Boston, MA: Beacon Press.

Messenger, John. 1983. *Inis Beag: Isle of Ireland*. Prospect Heights, IL: Waveland Press.

———. 1989. *Inis Beag Revisited: The Anthropologist as Observant Participator*. Salem, WI: Sheffield Publishing Company.

Middleton, John. 1965. *The Lugbara of Uganda*. Prospect Heights, IL: The Waveland Press.

Minneapolis Star-Tribune. 1994. "Scandal Flares Anew After Priest Dies in Dublin Bath House." November 11. Electronic document. http://news library.krmediastream.com.

Minuchin, Salvador. 1974. *Families and Family Therapy*. Cambridge, MA: Harvard University Press.

Moane, Geraldine. 1994. "A Psychological Analysis of Colonialism in an Irish Context." *Irish Journal of Psychology* 15:250–263.

Molnar, Augusta. 1982. "Women and Politics: Case of the Kham Magar of Western Nepal." *American Ethnologist* 9:485–502.

Moore, Barrington. 1984. *Privacy: Studies in Social and Cultural History*. Armonk, NY: M. E. Sharpe.

Morgan, D.H.J. 1975. *Social Theory and the Family*. London: Routledge & Kegan Paul.

Murdock, George P. 1949. *Social Structure*. New York: Macmillan.

Nelson, Cynthia. 1974. "Public and Private Politics: Women in the Middle Eastern World." *American Ethnologist* 1:551–563.

Ni Nuallain, M., A. O'Hare, and D. Walsh. 1990. "The Prevalence of Schizophrenia in Three Counties in Ireland." *Acta Psychiatrica Scandia* 82:136–140.

O'Brien, Joseph. 1982. *"Dear, Dirty Dublin": A City in Distress, 1899–1916*. Berkeley and Los Angeles: University of California Press.

O'Gorman, Paddy. 1994. *Queueing for a Living*. Dublin: Poolbeg.

O'Hanlon, Rory. 1995. "Statement on Abortion Information Bill." *Irish Times*, March 1, 1995: 3.

O'Reilly, Emily. 1992. *Masterminds of the Right*. Dublin: Attic Press.

Orfali, Kristina. 1991. "The Rise and Fall of the Swedish Model." In *A History of Private Life. Vol. 4. Riddles of Identity in Modern Times*. Antoine Prost and Gérard Vincent, eds. Pp. 417–449. Cambridge, MA: Belknap Press.

O Súilleabháin, Séan. 1967. *Irish Wake Amusements*. Cork: Mercier Press.

O'Sullivan, Kevin. 1998. "Mass Attendance Has Fallen to 60%, Survey Finds." *Irish Times*, February 4. Electronic document. http://www.irish-times. com/irish%2Dtimes/paper/1998/0204/hom3.html.

Ouroussoff, Alexandra. 1993. "Illusions of Rationality: False Premises of the Liberal Traditions." *Man* (n.s.) 28:281–298.

Parsons, T. and R. F. Bales. 1955. *Family, Socialization and Interaction Process*. Glencoe, IL: Free Press.

Patterson, Nerys. 1994. *Cattle-Lords and Clansmen: The Social Structure of Early Ireland*. 2d ed. Notre Dame, IN: University of Notre Dame Press.

Peacock, Nadine. 1991. "Rethinking the Sexual Division of Labor: Reproduction and Women's Work Among the Efe." In *Gender at the Crossroads of Knowledge: Feminist Anthropology in the Postmodern Era*. Micaela di

Leonardo, ed. Pp. 339–360. Berkeley and Los Angeles: University of California Press.

Phádraig, Máire Nic Ghiolla. 1976. "Religion in Ireland: Preliminary Analysis." *Social Studies* 5:116–119.

Pollak, Andy. 1996a. "A Dedicated, Outspoken Spiritual Leader." *Irish Times*, October 2. Electronic document. http://www.irish-times.com/irish%2Dtimes/paper/1996/1002/hom3.html.

———. 1996b. "Poll Shows Church's Moral Authority in Decline." *Irish Times*, December 16. Electronic document. http://www.irish-times.com/irish%2Dtimes/paper/1996/1216/hom42.html.

Pringle, Rosemary. 1994. "Office Affairs." In *Anthropology of Organizations*. Susan Wright, ed. Pp. 115–123. London: Routledge.

Prost, Antoine. 1991. "Public and Private Lives in France." In *A History of Private Life. Vol. 4. Riddles of Identity in Modern Times*. Antoine Prost and Gérard Vincent, eds. Pp. 3–143. Cambridge, MA: Belknap Press.

Quinn, Naomi. 1996. "Culture and Contradiction: The Case of American Reasoning About Marriage." *Ethos* 24:391–425.

Radcliffe-Brown A. R. 1965. *Structure and Function in Primitive Society: Essays and Addresses*. New York: Free Press.

Rapp, Rayna. 1982. "Family and Class in Contemporary America: Notes Toward an Understanding of Ideology." In *Rethinking the Family: Some Feminist Questions*. Barrie Thorne, ed., with Marilyn Yalom. Pp. 168–187. New York: Longman.

Reiter, Rayna R. 1975. "Men and Women in the South of France: Public and Private Domains." In *Toward an Anthropology of Women*. Rayna R. Reiter, ed. Pp. 252–282. New York: Monthly Review Press.

Robinson, Gary. 1997. "Families, Generations, and Self: Conflict, Loyalty, and Recognition in an Australian Aboriginal Society." *Ethos* 25:303–332.

Rogers, Susan Carol. 1975. "Female Forms of Power and the Myth of Male Dominance: A Model of Female/Male Interaction in Peasant Society." *American Ethnologist* 2:727–756.

Rosaldo, Michelle. 1974. "Woman, Culture, and Society: A Theoretical Overview." In *Woman, Culture, and Society*. Michelle Rosaldo and Louise Lamphere, eds. Pp. 17–42. Stanford, CA: Stanford University Press.

———. 1980. "The Use and Abuse of Anthropology: Reflections on Feminism and Cross-cultural Understandings." *Signs* 5:389–417.

Rubin, Lillian B. 1994. *Families on the Faultline: America's Working Class Speaks About the Family, the Economy, Race, and Ethnicity*. New York: HarperCollins.

Sacks, Karen B. 1984a. Introduction. In *My Troubles Are Going to Have Trouble with Me: Everyday Trials and Triumphs of Women Workers*. Karen B. Sacks and Dorothy Remy, eds. Pp. 1–12. New Brunswick, NJ: Rutgers University Press.

———. 1984b. "Generations of Working-class Families." In *My Troubles Are Going to Have Trouble with Me: Everyday Trials and Triumphs of Women Workers*. Karen B. Sacks and Dorothy Remy, eds. Pp. 15–38. New Brunswick, NJ: Rutgers University Press.

About the Author

ELIZABETH A. THROOP is Assistant Professor in the Department of Sociology, McKendree College, Lebanon, Illinois.